THE SECRET C
POWER & HOW TO USE IT

By
Dr. C. de RADWAN
(Ph.D. University of Vienna)

Founder and Scientific Adviser to the Radwan Institute of Psychology and Psychophony, London

Foreword by
Dr. ALEXANDER CANNON, k.c.a.
M.D., PH.D., D.P.M., M.A., F.R.S.

RIDER & CO., Paternoster House
Paternoster Row, London, E.C.4

Made and Printed in Great Britain at
The Mayflower Press, Plymouth. William Brendon & Son, Ltd

DR. C. DE RADWAN

Ph.D. (University of Vienna).

CONTENTS

6 CONTENTS

LIST OF ILLUSTRATIONS

DIAGRAMS

FOREWORD

IDEAS are things which you hold, but CONVIC-
TIONS are things which hold you. In my
opinion this book may contain many excellent
ideas, but of this I am certain, it is a conviction
which will grip the world in its clasp and lead
it from failure to SUCCESS, from sorrow to
JOY, from evil to GOOD, and bring home the
great truth that money can buy everything
except the KINGDOM OF GOD, which is within
each one of you.

This work removes, for ever, war; war
between thoughts which become things and
in time become war between peoples and
nations and destruction to the world, for which
Christ died that it might have peace. Herein
is found the secret path to peace, the way to
that Kingdom of Heaven that is within you,
and to health, wealth and happiness which
always follow in the way of peace, for the
Deity intended that all should have plenty,
more than enough.

I am very pleased with this book, but that

which is within it pleases me better. It is the result of much learning which shows how little most mortals know. Mollie Stanley Wrench, in her *Madness of Pan*, spoke well when she said : " Materialists may scoff or rage, we know the truth, who can

' Discern 'mid London's myriad sounds the madd'ning
    pipes of Pan.' "

Did not Una L. Silberrad, in her *Success*, say : " Nothing is impossible if you believe it can be done, but three-quarters of the world can neither believe nor do." My friend, Dr. de Radwan, has convincingly shown the reader why he must believe and why he "can do ! "

Marguerite Steen in *Matador* wrote : " To go through life only half-conscious of all that it offers you is the act of a fool." My belief is that in this book the reader will find that realization of consciousness which is so essential to the meaning of life.

" If God gives you wisdom, act on it, though the world and your friends call you mad," says Fletcher. Dr. de Radwan has given us that God-given vision through the greatest agency in the world, by a VIBRATION which the mind interprets as sound. His psychophony will do more for the world than all the Couéism we have known, good though this may be.

Dr. de Radwan has brought home in his psychophony some of the great truths which I have broadcast in *Powers That Be*, as, for example, on pages 96 and 97, I state : " If you do not rest you cannot work properly, and if you cannot work properly, you will never win success. Before you fall asleep at night (begin this very night to control your sleeping state), let every muscle of your body go flabby. Think of all these muscles as huge factories, employing millions of cell-men, and actually tell them to knock off their labours and take a rest. Most people go to sleep with their muscles taut—all the cells are keyed up and waiting for the body to resume its work, just as though they were workers in a factory who never were allowed to go home and enjoy relaxation, but were always kept in the factory by night and by day, ready to go on duty again. Think what a terrible strain such conditions would impose upon the workers ! They would soon break down in mind and body under the strain. In the same way do the little microscopic workers of the body need rest and peace if they are not to break down under the strain of life. When you have

learned to ' send all your workers home ' you
will be in a perfect state of relaxation. Your
legs will lie in effortless peace, and your head
will be loosely connected to the body—for the
neck muscles will be ' off duty.' Now breathe
deeply and evenly, remembering what I related
in a previous lecture about breath control, and
keep vividly in your mind the picture you
desire to materialize in your life-experience.
Think of the job you desire to attain to : the
love you wish to gain : the duty you wish to
undertake. Then, still fully relaxed and breathing deeply, you will fall asleep with this picture
held firmly in your mind. In the morning
you will awaken in a happy frame of mind :
ready to work well, and in absolute certainty
that the day will arrive when your dreams will
come true. Your certainty will be based upon
truth—for, indeed, your dreams must come
true."

In the preface to this same work, *Powers
That Be*, I wrote of the marvellous response
the world had given to *The Invisible Influence*,
which I wrote in 1933, and has indeed made its
presence felt from North to South, from East
to West, from Land's End to John o' Groats,
and from the Atlantic Coast to the Isle of
Thanet. The response was unbelievable and

unprecedented in its catholicity and its cosmo-
politanism. It was a miracle in itself. It
revealed to me that there was a growing army
of people, even in this materialistic Western
world, crying for this knowledge and for the
light. It showed me that, under the spurious
trappings of this false civilization, there burns
the ardour of men and women of the invisible
world and its influence. It makes clear to
me that there is a longing for the day when the
great truths so long buried in the East shall be
revealed to all men.

" I went to the most cosmopolitan centre I
could find," continues my preface to *Powers
That Be*, " the West End of London, and
there, as well as in our great University of
Oxford and other Seats of Learning, I gave
forth what I knew in the simplest and most
direct language I could find. In those lectures
I bore to the West testimony of the greater
knowledge of the East, that he who hath ears
might hear. I told my hearers of the Powers
That Be—powers which we, as sons of God,
have latent in us. I told them that we live in
a world incomparably greater than anything
imagined by Western science. I told them of
the wonders of the East, and of the marvels
of Eastern knowledge, of the power of Mind

over Matter.   Dr. C. de Radwan has clearly demonstrated this marvellous power in his " mind-power records," in which research I have played an active part, and which indeed comes as a boon and a blessing to all men.

Dr. de Radwan has not only made his student and disciple think aright by his psychophony, but he has enabled him to choose his mental designs carefully before he paints them upon the canvas of his mind.   If only the reader will follow this advice, which he is enforced to do as he listens to the forceful, persuasive voice from the records, his mental pictures will be painted with masterly strokes of power and decision ; the THOUGHT will then become the THING, and Life will, at last, be understood by a world which is now seething with unrest and seeking in vain for peace.   It will be realized that disease is dis-ease, dis-comfort ; a mind-body not at ease.   With ease and peace of mind, disease (dis-ease) will vanish for ever more. Herein, Dr. de Radwan reveals the way to true peace and happiness, to real power and to true greatness.

LONDON, W.1.   ALEXANDER CANNON.
    22nd June, 1935.

MOTTO

I am not dealing with anything new, and I make
no sensational promises. I do not set out any
scientific thesis. The practical is my sphere and
experience is my teacher. My methods place
science at the service of mankind, and the medium
which science recommends is created from practical experience, and for this reason inspires
confidence.

ACADEMIC KNOWLEDGE AND
PRACTICAL EXPERIENCE

BETWEEN the scholar in his study and the man in the street, between abstract science and everyday life there is an ever-widening gap.

For the ordinary person scientific theses cannot take the place of the metaphorical and poetical expressions of religion. Faith has been unable to withstand the attacks of positive science, and so these people, becoming wavering and uncertain in their faith, have lost the support on which they depended, and have been offered nothing of equal value to replace it. Science is above the heads of the ordinary mortal, and these facts probably help to explain the returning interest so many are evincing in magic and mysticism.

If man is to be helped he must be talked to in a simple and comprehensible language and given the use of the resources which science and practical experience have made known to us. The bridging of the gap between science and everyday life was the guiding idea in the

creation of a psychic system, which aims at
giving back the power of resistance and inner
harmony to those people who, in the present-
day critical conditions of life, forfeit what is
best.

THE SECRET OF MIND-POWER & HOW TO USE IT

BEHIND THE MASK OF THE PRESENT-DAY HUMAN

LET us forget for a moment the part we are playing on life's stage, and remove the mask we usually wear to disguise our true characters from ourselves and our fellow-men. In doing this we shall become aware of many unfortunate habits and stumble upon desires which we would not dare to disclose to our best friends. At the same time, we shall experience many surprises as far as others are concerned —those whom we meet every day. People whom we envy for their apparent efficiency, health and strength, prove to be just those who are lonely and thrown upon their own resources, and who are tormented by fear of the future, of poverty and death.

Crowds pass before our eyes, joyless, distrustful, and without any confidence, despondent and more or less broken by the crosses their souls have to carry. The best of us have to bear, in addition to personal burdens, the generally unsatisfactory conditions of the present day—*unemployment*, the effects of the world crisis, and political unrest and uncertainty, all of which have a crippling effect even on those not directly concerned. What is even more serious and fatal than the generally unsound situation is *the unhealthy and wrong-headed attitude of the majority towards it.*

Rightly understood, necessity is not an enemy but a friend. The popular saying describing it as the mother of invention is a true one. And not only that. She challenges our opposition, and makes us take stock of the rich arsenal of our outer and inner strength. By outward deprivation it leads us to inner enrichment, by temporary loss to permanent profit. Trouble only becomes our enemy when we allow it to alarm us, and when it causes us to lose courage and our sense of proportion and turns us into habitual grumblers. " Through grief we only make our cross and suffering greater," is a truth expressed in a popular hymn. Such a frame of mind dooms to failure our feeble attempts to overcome difficult circumstances and

LORD MOYNIHAN   DR. CANNON

that which we are unable either to cure or endure because we cannot summon up sufficient strength, assumes monstrous proportions in our imaginations and so still further diminishes our spiritual vigour.

This happens in small matters and in great. International endeavours and world conferences are wrecked for the reason that to every fresh attempt man brings the greatest mistrust. We all know how infectious that is. In the same way in which we speak of the self-made spiritual conditions of suffering individuals, it is possible to speak of sick nations and mankind in general, whose situation is aggravated by the general unsatisfactory conditions. That the general world depression may be traced to a type of mass-suggestion, and is, in fact, a psychic infection, is affirmed by some of the most prominent investigators of to-day. Even strong personalities suffer from the general wrong-headedness which must be looked upon as a psychic epidemic. Many of those who put a " good face " on it are psychically broken. If they consulted a doctor, he would have to say to them : " Your organs are sound, you are not ill." And yet these people, so deserving of pity, are tired of life, sick of life. The daily battle has used up their power of resistance. They can no longer wear the smiling mask the world demands. Lonely, they feel deep down in their souls the monster of fear threatening their lives. The greater the intellect, the greater the number of inner conflicts. The primitive man knew nothing of this. The tormenting of himself and others with all kinds of rules and regulations, and deterioration through a wrong manner of living and incorrect bodily and spiritual nourishment, is reserved for civilized man.

Psycho-analysis shows us how the whole energy of a person who has not the strength to bring about the fulfilment of his wishes is transformed into a nervous disease and in some cases into mental disease. In very many cases, turning one's back on one's work or one's task in life is the reaction called forth by the discord existing between one's personality and the demands of life.

" Neurasthenia," now rightly styled psychasthenia, is often a cloak to hide individual helplessness, an illusionary release from the burden of material worries and keeping up appearances. The present-day human often flees from life or fate. In this case he takes refuge in narcotics, whether it be morphia or something else. He stupefies himself in order to escape from everyday life and to experience the imaginary fulfilment of his wishes under intoxication.

Our generation, on which the sins of the World War are visited, alike on the descendants of the victors and the vanquished, is suffering from moral decay. The shadow of the world crisis darkens the fate of the individual, who, every day on waking, asks himself uneasily : " What will to-day bring ? "

In spite of the most refined civilization, man has never been so completely thrown on his own resources as he is to-day. His conscious mind has become worm-eaten with scepticism, and he is left alone, caught up in the net of inner conflicts.

THE RETURN TO INNER HARMONY

SUPPOSING one day we lost all our worldly goods, what would remain for us ? We should have those treasures, which man, blinded by materialism, has disregarded, the immeasurable powers which exist in the depths of our souls.

In reality we should always be healthy and happy because our nature is inclined to harmony and because a natural tendency for a balance of all functions rules in our system.

Our question should not be " What remedy will give us back our health, creative power and joy in living ? " but " How can we rid ourselves of all repressions, as we would release a brake, so that our natural tendencies may have their chance ? " The modern psyche may be likened to a motor driven with the brake on. The human of to-day is restricted in his undertakings and his activity, and cannot develop his full capacity. With nervous people, for example, those suffering from a fixation, the greater portion of their energy is absorbed

by the fixation, and, therefore, it is not surprising that they are incapable of any great
performance.   In such cases, the virtue of
their energy is impaired, not by its insuffi-
ciency, but by its FALSE APPLICATION.

At a time of general degeneration, Jean
Jacques Rousseau demanded a return to
nature: we, in a time of spiritual decadence,
should demand A RETURN TO THE SOUL
AND TO INNER HARMONY.   Plants and flowers
turn to the sun.   Why should our endeavours
not be towards the inward light and inner
harmony?   Each one of us is responsible
if he does not take to heart the importance of
the correct functioning of his psychic motor
or neglects his psychic structure.   There are
only two possibilities in life, to be the anvil
or the hammer, the master or the servant.
Awaken to action!   The sun shines for all,
and everyone has an equal right to a full life
and real happiness.   Deliverance lies in ourselves, in the immeasurable powers of our own
soul.

THE SPIRITUAL WEAPON

IF we go back in thought to the time of primitive man we encounter the " Magician," the first witch-doctor, who cures the sick through incantations. As far back as the time of ancient Greece, priests in the temples healed through suggestion and hypnosis. Still further back we find them being used by the Chinese and Egyptians, and before that by the Atlantians prior to the year 254,666 B.C.

The recognition that the faith of the sick in the remedies prescribed and in the personality of the doctor brings about a cure is like a red thread running through the history of medicine. When the same thing occurs at a place of pilgrimage like Lourdes, where the personality of the doctor is eliminated, we may gauge the large part played by hetero- and auto-suggestion in the cures.

In the last few years eminent scientists, such as van Renterghem, Moll, Bergson, Dessoir, Janet, Freud, Jung and Cannon, have verified that psychic power exists in reality, and that cures can be achieved through psychic influence. The present-day practical psychology talks of two provinces of the soul, the CONSCIOUS MIND, with which man has long been familiar, and the SUBCONSCIOUS MIND, which has only been penetrated in recent years, and is part of the unconscious mind. Will is an activity of the conscious mind, while hetero- and auto-suggestion concern the subconscious mind. Let us consider these forces in detail.

(a) WILL-POWER

The scientific scholars of the Middle Ages looked upon the will as a special organ of the human soul, with which man was provided, ready-made, at birth. The modern psychologists, on the contrary, believe that will-power may be developed through methodical mental exercises. For practical purposes, let us compare our will-power with a large factory. Our activities would be the products made by the engines and machines, while the image of the goal to be reached corresponds to the plan of the management. To possess a will means to have an aim before one, to have clearly before one all the stages leading to the realization of the aim, and to have sufficient energy to overcome all obstacles which one may find in one's way. " I will—I can," is the motto of the strong-willed man, who understands how to use activity to the greatest advantage in order to attain his object.

WHAT OBSTACLES DO WE ENCOUNTER MOST FREQUENTLY ON THE ROAD TO THE STRENGTHEN-ING OF OUR WILL-POWER ? Let us suppose we are dealing with a man whose will-power is hampered by nervousness. How can we expect strength of purpose from him, when his brain is governed by brooding, doubt and fear ?

Let us consider general nervousness. It would not be suitable here to discuss the general causes of present-day nervousness. It is sufficient to emphasize that every aggrava-tion of the fight for existence increases the contrast between what we demand of life and what life offers. In any case, PRESENT-DAY NERVOUSNESS ORIGINATES FROM THE SUPPRES-SION OF OUR EMOTIONS AND DESIRES, for the fulfilment of which we have not the courage.

WHAT ATTRIBUTES ARE REQUIRED IN ORDER TO BECOME A STRONG-WILLED INDIVIDUAL ? COURAGE, SELF-CONFIDENCE and PERSEVERANCE.

The strong-willed man must possess COUR-AGE. In traversing a narrow defile of the St. Bernard Pass, Napoleon asked one of his officers if it were possible to go through the pass, to which the soldier replied : " Perhaps it is not impossible." " Forward, then ! " ordered the general. We should always have this answer in mind when obstacles make us waver on the way to our goal. In order to be strong-willed one must banish the image of fear for ever from one's soul, and always be prepared to sacrifice one's life to a high aim.

We must become familiar with danger by calling up in our imagination situations of ever-increasing difficulty, so that at the critical moment the soul reacts rightly.

SELF-CONFIDENCE is like good oil, without which our psychic motor cannot function. How can one influence others, when one does not feel sure of oneself ? We should diffuse self-confidence and evoke a feeling of security in our surroundings. " My lord, do you know that I alone am in a position to save the country, and that no one else is capable of it ? " are the words which Pitt in 1757 spoke to the reigning prince. We must be filled with the same self-confidence, for there is no more compelling force than that which comes from conviction.

PERSEVERANCE is a precious attribute for the strong-willed man. The attainment of one's wishes depends on it. Even genius cannot achieve anything really great and lasting without perseverance, while a man with but slight talents and little strength can achieve a high aim through perseverance. Perseverance is like the eternal starlight in comparison with the fireworks of sudden impulses. We must always keep in mind that it is of greater importance patiently to overcome the vexations of everyday life with courage and perseverance than occasionally to perform some great feat. The daily repetition of the words : " I am calm and I can wait," is the best means of cultivating will-power.

How can one develop will-power and turn it into a psychic tractor ? On what is based the development of our will ? On the regular and methodical practice of all functions depending on the will. Will-power is dependent on the repetition of the exercises, and is finally founded on the appropriate reactions being performed automatically by the psychic mechanism. A man with well-cultivated will-power may be likened to a workman who is able to achieve a maximum of execution with a minimum of exertion.

As already observed, cultivation of the will depends on methodical practice, in which we may differentiate the general and the particular. We can improve the whole range of our will-power, or perfect ourselves in one special province, as circumstances dictate. The desirability of and need for will development and the roads to it are, to the majority, still far too little known, though there is a general conviction of the significance of psychic culture, and a perception that appropriate exercises are one of the chief mediums for achieving it. Many do not understand that mental faculties, like muscles, suffer atrophy when they are not regularly used. In general it is realized how much may be done through regular exercises to remove fatigue and to improve the concentration and memory. Dr. Alexander Cannon has proved that " Memory depends on relaxation. If a person is tense in attitude, the memory fails."

Less well-known are the results of psychic drill with " autogen-organic " exercises. Dr. Schulz has proved that the heart, the muscles of the intestines, and the action of the glands as well as the temperature can be influenced and regulated. In connection with the curve of progress it is interesting to note the fact that a period of fairly rapid progress is followed by an interval of rest. In such cases further

c

advancement may be achieved by the awaken-
ing of a new interest. These considerations
make it appear advisable to commence the
development of the will with the most simple
exercises and gradually to proceed to more
complicated ones. Daily repetition will make
the exercises second nature to us. *Mere
knowledge of the exercises is not enough ; they
must also be performed methodically.* Here we
are approaching the province of psychic life.
The human being of to-day recognizes the
value of mental training, but has not sufficient
vitality to carry it out methodically. This is
the " black point " where previous methods
have failed.

(*b*) AUTO-SUGGESTION

Auto-suggestion is frequently discussed
to-day, and it is often believed that it is a
discovery of modern psychology because in
this connection it is often forgotten that
man is born with a susceptibility to suggestion.

Without the suggestibility, which each one
of us possesses, and the capacity to have faith
and be influenced, art and religion could not
have existed. From the cradle to the grave,
suggestion plays a great part in our lives.

Dr. Alexander Cannon in his book, *Hypnotism, Suggestion and Faith-healing*, writes as follows :

" Suggestion is most powerful in its action upon the mind of man in the hypnotic state, and it must not be forgotten that we live by suggestion. We dress according to the clothes suggested by advertisements ; we try to keep up with the times ; all this means that we act upon the suggestions of others (hetero-suggestion) ; I have found the bottle of medicine do as much good to a patient when a chemist has accidentally omitted to place in it the ' all-important ' ingredient. Of course there are exceptions, but facts cannot be altered."

During our upbringing, teacher, family and environment are the decisive influences in the formation of our characters. Whether it is a question of political, financial or social matters, we live in a suggestive atmosphere, like fish in water. We do not realize it because auto-suggestion is a product of the subconscious mind. We see results without understanding how they are arrived at. We often ask ourselves what this unknown power in our souls really is. We encounter it when we have suddenly forgotten a name or mislaid an object, and, despite every effort of will, cannot succeed in setting our memory in action ; and yet in such cases it is sufficient to give up worrying over it and return to work or take up an interrupted conversation, and we once again have the information we desired. It was the subconscious mind which placed the recollection on the surface of our conscious mind, in the same way as the ocean throws up mussels from the deep on to the shore. How often we believe that we have once before seen a person, without being able to give an account to ourselves of the time, place and circumstances.

The subconscious mind governs all vaso-motor functions. Normal heart action depends on it ; it regulates the secretion of the glands, the circulation of the blood, breathing and digestion. At its instigation we draw away our fingers from a burning object before we have felt it. The subconscious mind calls forth an unconscious reaction to guard us from a danger, before we have become aware of it. This subconscious mind is far more powerful than our conscious will. In us, then, is a force which works unseen like the ship's engines under the decks, and, like the ship's passengers, we are only aware of its existence through seeing the results of its working.

With suggestive activity we can only be

sure of one thing, and it is that the subconscious mind can be set in motion by a vivid representation, and every result of this is evoked in the same way as various articles are released from an automatic machine by the insertion of coins. In this the person under the influence of auto-suggestion has no idea of the working of the machine of the subconscious mind. If we are asked what auto-suggestion is, we can define it as the taking place of sensations, emotions and acts of will under *inadequate conditions*, that is, we experience perceptions without physiological provocation, make judgments without good reasons, and practice acts of will without real motives.

Dr. Cannon, in *The Principles and Practice of Psychiatry*, writes as follows :

" Many psychologists believe that there may be some cupboards there which, whilst they are not open, we have a vague idea of their contents ; these cupboards represent what is often termed the subconscious mind. The remaining cupboards represent what is termed the true unconscious mind, in that their contents are not known, until by some means or other those cupboards are opened. Napoleon used to speak of his mind as containing many cupboards. He used to say that when he wanted to think about something more pleasant he used to shut up those particular cupboards and open up others. That when he wanted to go to sleep, he would shut up all the cupboards of his mind.

" It is clear that there are many thoughts in our mind to which the cupboard door gets somehow closed, and these for a time can be recalled by an effort, as one still remembers the contents of that particular cupboard ; this explains the comparative ease with which some of the cupboards can be searched, and hence the subconscious thoughts quickly become conscious. In everyday life this can be shown by the fact that whilst gazing at a watch the onlooker is somehow reminded of an appointment he has to keep to-morrow at the same time in the morning. Again, I ask you who is the Chancellor of the University, and instantly you become aware of his name. All these memories are revived from the subconscious mind. On the other hand, the true unconscious is represented by the thoughts penned up in those closed cupboards whose contents we are not aware of, and unless by accident or for some reason or other, unknown to us, the door of any one of those closed cupboards is opened to us, we are unable to name the contents of those thoughts ; this represents the thoughts of the true unconscious mind, which may lie dormant for years, maybe for ever, but nevertheless in some way or other influence the recording of the more accessible thoughts and so affect our conscious life without us knowing it. We have a caretaker called the censor, who sees to it that certain cupboards shall not be opened if he can help it. The unconscious mind is frequently spoken of as the primary or primitive system, and the conscious mind as the secondary system.

" The unconscious mind is seen most unmistakably at work in dreams, in the distorting mechanisms of condensation, or the fusion of images ; dramatization, or the unique and camouflaged picturing of the facts ; displacement which assists in the camouflaging of the picture by displacing the importance of certain facts ; and after the dream is over the process of *secondary elaboration* which is the final safeguard against letting out the real meaning of the dreams by consciousness attempting to make a nice connected account of what the individual has dreamt, and in so doing unconsciously omitting the minor important points where the true nature of the dream-thoughts disguise was dangerously thin. The whole process is quite unconscious and is no deliberate falsification on the part of the dreamer.

" Among other mental mechanisms under phantasy, we have spoken of dreaming of ' castles in the air ' ; do not forget to bring them down to Mother Earth. Make the psychological reality a physical reality wherever possible. You dream of a great future, and I can assure you that it is within your power to make those dreams come true. *This is how you can do it.* Whatever you are called upon to do should receive your whole-hearted attention and interest—your maximum ability. Do it in such a way that those above you will take notice. You can compel them to notice you if only you have enough vigour and common sense. It depends upon you. To become despondent about your lot in life is to belittle yourself : to be determined on greater things will surely bring its reward. In gauging your own importance do not allow yourself to float in a sea of superlative egotism ; in other words, do not let your head swell ! A proper estimate of oneself must include credit for retaining control. When you realize your own importance you will keep control of it, so that you may apply your power in a sensible and cool way. You are bigger than you think you are. Act up to this. Then as the years go by you will bring your 'castles in the air' down to the reality of Mother Earth, and your dreams will be interpreted in a very realistic way ; indeed, your dreams will then come true. You will then be a living psychologist who can put into practice the theory which you teach."

The tragedy in this connection is that human nature is far more accessible to bad unconscious hetero- and auto-suggestion than to good conscious suggestion. Therefore, we often see people, who live in perpetual fear of their immediate future, who cause themselves un-necessary anxiety and who even in their dreams are tormented by terrifying forebodings. And the worst of it is that in time there is built up an auto-suggestive resistance to everything which could deliver them from this spiritual poisoning. Unconscious auto-suggestion can not only produce phenomena of nervous origin, but even organic disease. It also renders medical diagnosis more difficult, and can even falsify the symptoms and lead to a false diagnosis. Auto-suggestion can cause the greatest harm to our system, but, rightly applied, can become the greatest blessing for furthering our well-being, success, productive powers, contentment and joy of living.

The most popular acceptance by the public of the practical application of auto-suggestion is found in Coué's world-famous formula : " Every day and in every way I am better and better."

However, practice has shown that, where self-influence is concerned, the capacity of the individual has been often over-estimated, and that the present-day human is frequently no longer able to concentrate successfully.

THE INADEQUACY OF EARLIER
PSYCHIC METHODS

IT has already been observed that training of the will and many other psychic practices lead to a cul-de-sac, and that the present-day " nerve-ridden " individual is incapable of continuing the exercises. Many failures may be traced to lack of concentration and lack of perseverance. To find a reliable method we should put our trust in nature and obey her laws.

Let us consider the bad habits of heavy drinking, inordinate smoking and morphia-taking. The people addicted to these vices did not become slaves to them suddenly. Step by step, the habits won a hold in their souls, and it is the strength—originating in repetition—of the habit which has enslaved them. The habit has not entered through the open door of the conscious mind, but has slunk up the backstairs of the subconscious mind.

I have noticed particularly with morphia

addicts the way in which strong-willed individuals, after repeated injections, find themselves
caught in the net of habit. Usually the first
injection is made to obtain relief from pain.
Its recurrence is an occasion for a repetition
of the injection, and soon the slightest irritation
induces the subject to continue the use of the
drug. WHY SHOULD WE NOT TAKE A LESSON
FROM BAD HABITS, AND TURN THE SAME POWER
OF REPETITION TO OUR ADVANTAGE, when a
technical resource is at our service, and we are
in a position mechanically to produce repetition which will induce good habits ? Add to
this the fact that all day long we are affected
by slight, unconscious impressions, and are
dependent on this mental atmosphere, and the
question presents itself peremptorily why we
should not turn all this methodically to our
advantage.

WHAT IS PSYCHOPHONY?

WE have already referred to the inadequacy of various psychic methods and the power of repetition.

Experience teaches that a suggestion must always be carried out with the same suggestive strength in order to be effective. If it is repeated only by the individual while in a condition of depression it remains more or less ineffective. One cannot expect of the present-day human a sufficient concentration to see that the necessary conditions are fulfilled, any more than one could expect a financier to undertake the management of a large business which had no capital. Practice has proved that it is illogical to demand from a person performances of which he is incapable. To make use of a comparison from the realms of locomotion, earlier psychic methods may be described as a pedal cycle, while psychophony is like the powerful car, which only requires starting to run on its own power. In order to set the mechanism of the subconscious mind

in motion, we have made use of hetero-
suggestion in the so-called " mind-power "
records. The place of the suggestionist is
taken by the picture of the staring eyes and
the voice from the gramophone. Very sensitive
people have expressed the feeling that the
presence of the suggestionist has a disturbing
effect on the suggestion, and the thought of
subjugating their will to another arouses an
unpleasant sensation in them, while the above-
mentioned picture and the voice from the
gramophone scarcely rouse any opposition or
negativism. In working on psychophony, this
was taken into consideration.

ON WHAT IS PSYCHOPHONY BASED ?

PYTHAGORAS, the Greek philosopher, who flourished about the year 562 B.C., taught the greatest truth known to the world, that everything in the Universe, everything we see, everything we hear, everything we feel, vibrates. As regards these vibrations, we know that the difference between ice, water and steam is purely a matter of alteration in the vibrations of two atoms of hydrogen and one of oxygen. The difference between iron and wood is merely a difference in the vibrations of the particles of the invisible ether contained in the two objects. In like manner the difference between happiness and misery is a question of alterations in mind-vibrations. DR. ALEXANDER CANNON, describes these facts in detail in his book, *The Invisible Influence*. Pythagoras also showed that the alteration in this invisible ether can be made by sound vibrations, and when a person speaks or sings, he not only sets in motion air vibrations,

47

which affect the mechanism of hearing, but also sets a vibration working in the invisible ether which passes through people's bodies and brains, thereby affecting the mental state of those who come within its reach.

In the psychophonic system the gramophone records do not only reproduce the sound vibrations of the speaker, the suggestionist and the hypnotist, as well as those of the musician who plays the music, but ALSO CONVEY IN THE INVISIBLE ETHER A PSYCHIC VIBRATION, IDENTICAL WITH THAT OF THE SUGGESTIONIST'S MIND, a special system, discovered by DR. de RADWAN, having to be used to ensure this result. BY THIS TECHNIQUE THE MIND-POWER IS CONTAINED WITHIN THE PSYCHOPHONIC RECORD. In that way each time it is played, not only are the verbal and musical sounds reproduced, but also the mind-power of the suggestionist in the vibrations, which are again sent out upon the invisible ether each time the special record is played.

In this way the ancient knowledge of Pythagoras is applied in the most modern form of psychophony, and in this way, for the first time in the existence of the present world, the special mind-power vibrations which you require are reproduced on the invisible ether,

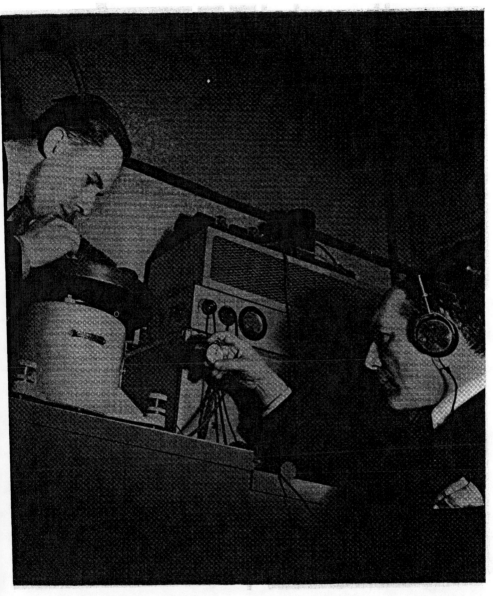

DR. DE RADWAN (RIGHT) TIMING A MIND-POWER RECORD FOR CORRECT
SPEED TO PRODUCE THE MAXIMUM SUGGESTIVE POWER

at your command, by the use of the psychophonic records. As a result of this and the
subtle influence of the voice from the record,
the daily repetition will make an ever-increasing and lasting impression upon your mind,
with astonishing and pleasing results. The
method is founded on the psychological principle of the ENERGY OF REPETITION. Even the
most refractory person can be influenced in
this way.

Here are some pictures illustrating the technique of procedure :

1. Dr. de Radwan influences a trained person,
whom, after some weeks of preparation, he
puts into a deep hypnotic trance.

2. The medium in a trance makes the record
for each individual.

3. Dr. de Radwan supervises the resulting
records, many of which are destroyed before
the correct and most efficacious one is produced.

4. Special Record for insomnia.

THE MERITS OF THIS MECHANICAL METHOD
OF SUGGESTION ARE BASED ON THE FACT THAT
EACH PERSON, ACCORDING TO HIS REQUIRE-
MENTS, CAN REPEAT THE RECORDS AT WILL,

D

AND FURTHER HE IS NOT RESTRICTED IN THEIR
USE TO A CERTAIN TIME AND PLACE.

Owing to this discovery, the inner protective properties of the subconscious mind are
set in motion and no efforts on the part of the
person concerned are necessary, as the desired
results are arrived at without his knowledge.

The sceptic will ask : " How can psychic
influence, the spoken word, effect suggestion
through records ? "

Recently the well-known Frankfurt nerve
specialist, Dr. Oppenheim, announced to
medical circles in Frankfurt that he had
obtained good results with records, and that he
had transferred the actual vibrations of the
records to the patients.

Why should not mechanical suggestion lie
within the realm of possibility ? When the
reproduced voice of a singer calls up various
emotions in us, when certain music causes our
hearts to beat more quickly, why should it not
be possible to obtain the same effect by reproduced suggestion ? Nevertheless, in practice
we stumbled upon great difficulties, and, in
order to transfer not mere words, but actual
suggestions, we have worked out a method
and made records, whose object is to control
this self-influence and lead it to a successful

execution ; this wish has been completely fulfilled.

This is not the place to discuss this method in detail. One thing must always be remembered. The suggestion formulæ must be rhythmic, which is only natural, as suggestive influence is based to a great extent on rhythm. Further, the suggestions must be as far as possible spoken in the same tone of voice, because the changing of the tone can easily rouse and disturb the person who is being influenced.

The chief difficulty lies in the correct composition of the suggestion formulæ, for it is to be remembered in this connection that what can pass unnoticed when it is a case of personal influence is turned to caricature when it is repeated a hundred times. Whether a word is repeated once or many times is often of the greatest moment. The most important suggestions must stand out like the predominating colour in a painting. I was fortunate to get the collaboration of Dr. Cannon in this matter, and together we have made great studies in this direction.

After each daily repetition the listener will be more and more strongly influenced by the subtle compulsion of the imperative voice proceeding from the gramophone, so that in this way the enormous energy of the repetition resembles a stream, the flow of which is regulated, and which man can turn to his use.

After a certain time the daily repetition of this psychic injection causes the individual to succumb to the exhortation of the mind-power records, so that EVEN THE MOST SCEPTICAL AND REFRACTORY PERSON may be influenced in this way. One person requires a great number of repetitions, another is influenced after quite a short period. THIS METHOD DEMANDS NO EFFORT OF WILL and no special concentration, because the action becomes purely mechanical through frequent repetition. It is not necessary to believe in the efficacy of the mind-power records ; it is only necessary to play them.

One of the GREAT ADVANTAGES of the psychophonic influence is that the command once given, the subject can receive it in a PURELY MECHANICAL fashion as often as he pleases, and that the DAILY REPETITION at home ENSURES A LASTING RESULT, which is not always the case in hypnotic treatment, because the patient, as soon as he is removed from the range of the hypnotist's influence, may lose confidence and in time falls easily into a relapse. The efficacy of the psychophonic records increases daily and each month the favourable results become more and more noticeable. That everybody can obtain RESULTS THROUGH DISTANT TREATMENT without leaving his home or interrupting his professional work is a further merit of psychophony. In spite of all these advantages of the mind-power records, we emphasize the necessity, in serious cases, of a diagnosis and treatment by a doctor of medicine, when the psychophonic records should then be used only as an aid or as an after treatment.

We first applied psychophony on receiving a letter from a student in South America, in which he related that the good effect of my influence abated considerably after my departure. At that time we transferred the same suggestion formula to a gramophone record and sent it to South America. The result far exceeded our expectations. The repetition over a period of months led to a lasting success.

ON WHAT DEPENDS THE EFFECT OF THE MIND-POWER RECORDS ?

In the Greek temples the patients, who were to be hypnotized by the priests, underwent a special preparation. They had to fast for the whole day. They were then allowed a glimpse from the temple steps of the results of healing. The correct preparation also plays an important part in psychic influence. Just as the earth must be prepared by the plough before the sowing takes place, so must the soul be prepared for the reception of the mechanical suggestion. Our first records, which contained only verbal suggestions, did not succeed completely. Gradually we created the suitable conditions by empirical means. The new subjects were first invited to read a synopsis of the methods and to watch the effect of the records on others by being present at psychophonic sittings. Before using the records, the subject must look at the picture of the staring eyes for about a minute, at the same time breathing deeply and regularly. These preparations have proved to be good in practice.

To achieve the full effect of the mind-power records, the suggestion must penetrate by all the doors of the senses. We know from everyday experience that, if we wish to fix something in our memory over a long period, it is wise to connect the image we are concerned with, with visual, auditory and other impressions of the senses. So that in the further development of psychophony the verbal suggestions are combined with appropriate music, which puts the soul in a suitable mood. We all know how much influence music exercises on our system. A gay tune is sufficient to make our faces light up and put us in a cheerful frame of mind. As well as music, suitable lighting is made use of, in which connection it may be remarked that, for instance, red light excites, while blue light soothes. By these several means, the spoken word, rhythm and light, the human soul is transformed into a state of heightened receptivity. It is not necessary to trouble oneself about the way in which one's wishes are realized through the medium of the records, or how the mechanical instigation of the subconscious mind produces the results.

It is a well-known psychological fact that everything which is repeated in a uniform manner in the conscious mind in time becomes mechanized or automatic in action : that is, it is reproduced time after time without participation of the attention or without an impulse of will. On the contrary, the attention and the will restrict and disturb the regular current of the psychic flow. Habit, in fact every activity from speech to the skill of genius, is based on this. Following this psychological fact, in the course of time the psychic mechanism, created by the daily repetition of the psychophonic records, produces the required reaction in the face of fresh evils as they appear, in the same way as the body produces reflex actions. Thus it is unnecessary to believe in the efficacy of psychophony : one merely has to repeat the playing of the records frequently, their action being a purely mechanical one. It is not necessary to believe in electric light : it is sufficient to turn on the switch in order to obtain light.

THE GENERAL PSYCHOPHONIC SYSTEM

THE best mind-power records would be useless without the perfected system, which gives the present-day human an inner discipline and offers him a steadiness and a healthy psychic attitude for the whole day. We have more than once emphasized that it is chiefly a lack of inner discipline which causes the present-day human to break down. He is like a ship without a rudder, lives without any high ideals, without any real aim in life, and is like a derelict ship, at the mercy of the wind and waves. The motive power—religion, faith in God and harmony with the infinite—has been taken from him. In order to provide everyone —whatever their creed, whether they have faith or not—with inner discipline, to help them to inner harmony, to give them back their lost confidence, we have worked out a system, which is adapted to life rhythm, and which, thanks to the systematic psychic influence, builds up a healthy regime of life and

a daily discipline. Therefore we have divided
up these influences accordingly.

THE MORNING OF ENERGY RECORD is to be
used immediately on rising and is a form of
psycho-gymnastics, with the object of " crank-
ing up " the individual for the daily work, and
providing him with fresh strength and
" psychic vitamins."

THE AFTERNOON OR RELAXING RECORD, is
played in the afternoon and serves to soothe
and relax the nerves. Its task is to disconnect
the psychic motor.

THE EVENING OR REGENERATION RECORD, used
just before going to sleep, sets the inner
protective powers in motion to the benefit
of the individual.

This diagram shows the actions of the
morning, afternoon and evening records. The
tests were carried out by Dr. Alexander Cannon
with the help of the Psychograph, or Thought-
Reading Machine, which he has invented.

First on the diagram are very irregular lines
indicating mind-wandering, followed by lines
representing visual thought while the subject
looks at a picture. The upward pointing
arrow after this shows the commencement of
the playing of Part 1 of the morning record,
played at a speed of 80, and the downward-

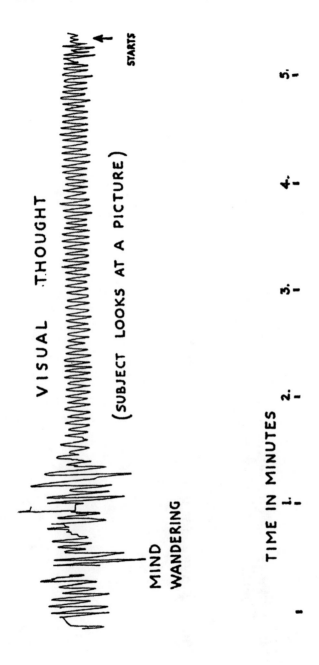

DR. C. DE RADWAN'S "MORNING RECORD"
Part I. played (at 80)

FINISHES STARTS

DR. C. DE RADWAN'S "MORNING RECORD"

MIND FINISHES

Part 2. played (at 80)
[but subject did not practice
the exercises and only imagined
he was doing them]

6.   7.   8.   9.   10.   11.

pointing arrow marks its conclusion. The second upward-pointing arrow denotes the commencement of Part 2 of the morning record, also played at a speed of 80, and the second downward-pointing arrow is its conclusion. It is to be noted that, in the playing

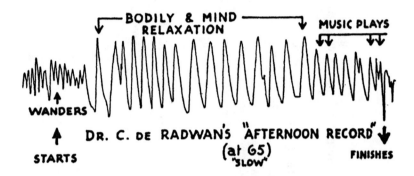

of this record, the subject in this case did not practise the exercises of the record as is usual, but only imagined he was doing them. Now comes a short period of mind-wandering before the commencement of the afternoon record, indicated by the fifth arrow. The sixth arrow shows the conclusion of the afternoon record,

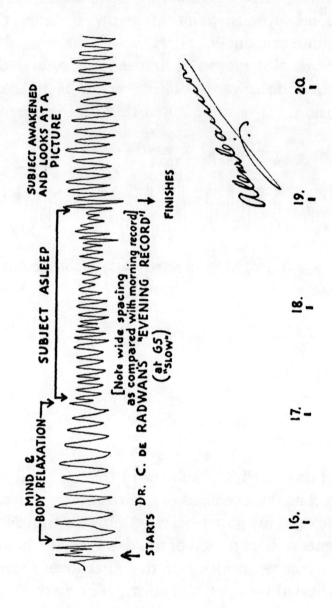

which is played at the slow speed of 65. The last two arrows represent the commencement and conclusion of the evening record, during the latter portion of which the subject is asleep. This record is also played at a speed of 65. The difference in the width of the spacing of the lines between the morning and evening records is to be observed, showing complete relaxation, those of the evening one being much wider and deeper. At the conclusion of the evening record the subject is awakened and again looks at a picture, giving once more, for comparison, the usual type of psychographic record.

PSYCHIC RENOVATION

REMEMBER that when your motor-car has run so many thousand miles, you send it to be overhauled. Why should you not do the same with your psychic motor and undergo a psychic renovation by means of the general mind-power records ? In one word : WITH THIS PSYCHOPHONIC SYSTEM EVERYONE CAN RESTORE HIS SELF-CONTROL AND POWERS OF RESISTANCE, HIS CONFIDENCE AND HIS COURAGE, AND WIN BACK HIS INNER HARMONY AND CONTENTMENT, as well as renew bodily vigour. Consider ; after all, on what is human happiness based ? Without doubt on the feeling of inner satisfaction. The possibility of inner satisfaction lies in everybody's nature. However, in these times it is stunted by all kinds of repressions, and it is psychophony's principle task to aid this delicate plant. If we look back at our past life we must come to the conclusion that everything in life is dependent on the spiritual attitude. There is no situation which is too difficult to overcome. There are only people who react falsely, and therefore we see that it ⸴is better to possess confidence and courage than to own stocks and shares which only too often suffer depreciation and become so much worthless paper. In the fight for existence, instead of tormenting ourselves and wearing ourselves out for the sake of more or less illusionary possessions, we should do far better to acquire inner harmony and contentment by the use of the psychophonic system. To-day man toils and moils far too much to pile up money, and with it buy longed-for objects, which he thinks will bring him contentment. It would be simpler and wiser to begin at the root of the matter, with contentment itself. It is easier to win back inner harmony and return to simplicity than to accumulate money, and it is more reasonable to take pleasure in the blue sky and enjoy the aromatic air of the mountains than to overload the stomach and spend much money on empty worldly pleasures.

Is THERE A MIND-POWER RECORD WHICH IS A DIRECT MEANS OF FILLING OUR PURSES ? Certainly not ; but by means of the psychophonic system our self-confidence and our influence over others will be strengthened to such an

E

extent that by these indirect means we are able to improve our material position.

And the effect in the home, or in the trenches of the daily battle for existence ? The irritable individual, the harassed business man and the discontented woman are products of the times with which everyone is familiar. A wit has said that to-day 105 per cent are nervous, irritable, moody and depressed, and, so far as specially sensitive natures are concerned, they are all well on the way to nervous disease. They arrive home, strained and vexed with the day's work, can take pleasure in nothing, are easily provoked, and infect their circle with their bad temper. Before it comes to this, take refuge in psychophony. Throw yourself in the nearest arm-chair, set the gramophone going and a deep vibrating voice will envelop you in a mantle of well-being. Your nerves relax and are soothed. You forget your irritations and worries. When the record has finished playing you will find you are in a cheerful and contented frame of mind. You may shake your head and laugh sceptically ; nevertheless this is the result when you have repeated the records with sufficient frequency, and allowed them to work through your subconscious mind.

THE INDIVIDUAL PSYCHOPHONIC
INFLUENCE

THE effect of suggestion is based on individualization. Just as there are no two leaves exactly alike, so there are no two personalities just alike. For different people it is necessary, in addition to general records, to use different records, adapted to their special needs. In this way the general psychophonic system forms a suitable foundation for the treatment of each person, while the individual record is adapted to their particular character and serves the realization of their particular desires. For those interested, a special mind-power record will be made in the laboratory, based on a " psychophonic test." The composition of such an individual record is very difficult and success is entirely dependent on it. The formulæ must express the wishes in the form of positive commands and the style be that of a telegram. For example, the formula : " I am not nervous, because I will not be nervous," from two points of view is utterly wrong. In this case the correct formula would be : " Every day my nerves are becoming stronger and calmer, stronger and calmer, stronger and calmer." In this way the formula must contain the appropriate idea. Our subconscious mind is like a labourer, to whom instructions must be given in the simplest and most easily comprehensible language possible. Years of experience are required for the composition of the psychophonic records, and so psychophonic individual influence is only possible through an Institute, whose students are for months under expert supervision, and can rely in every way on the assistance of the most skilled and experienced guidance.

PREVENTION

PREVENTION (not only cure) is psychophony's first task. We know that we are carriers of millions of minute lives, the cells and so-called microbes, which can produce dreaded diseases in us. It is the inner protective powers which shield us from this fate. Disease originates at the moment when the resisting power of our system yields to the attacks of infection. This explains the fact that, during an epidemic, those who are afraid of illness are the first to fall victims to it. Recently in a well-known medical clinic, experiments with white mice were performed, which showed that those animals in which a state of terror had been induced succumbed to disease quicker and more easily than any others. Therefore, for the preservation of health it is necessary to cultivate powers of resistance while one feels in good health. Medical history confirms this, for it proves that physical as well as mental hygiene has an advantage over artificially made medicines. So the mind-power records aim in the first place at strengthening our powers of resistance, and mobilizing our inner protective forces. In this way we attain a psychic insurance against infection and depression, and prevent premature ageing. Why are fatal attacks of apoplexy and so-called angina pectoris the order of the day ? Because, through wrong physical and psychic nourishment, we have done everything to injure our constitution, to raise the blood-pressure and cause nervous disorders. Why should we not absorb a kind of psychic vitamins through the mind-power records in the same way as we would take a diet, and in this way preserve our health, youth and beauty ? We can look on this suggestive action as a mobilization order through the mind-power records. It is of the greatest importance that through this the reserves of energy are set in motion.

SELF-MASTERY

IN these times it is not possible to overrate the importance of calm and strong nerves in every phase of life. How rare are those people who, in the worst situations, are able to control their thoughts and emotions. How many of them lose the desire and courage to live when some astrologer, fortune-teller or soothsayer has predicted a gloomy future for them. The most dangerous type to-day is the pessimist, always predicting the worst, whose spirit is soaked through with poisonous thoughts, and whose influence on his surroundings is more deadly than the most dangerous infectious disease : and all those who create unnecessary worries for themselves, who become restless and cannot sleep any more because they are unable to free themselves from gloomy thoughts, are really healthy and efficient, and only suffer from false imaginings.

How much family happiness and domestic peace has been wrecked through lack of self-control, because a woman cannot rouse herself from a preoccupation with what is petty, or a man is unable to shake off business worries and depression before he arrives home. How dissatisfied we are with ourselves, how dissatisfied others are with us, how much regret and remorse is suffered because we desire what is good but cannot attain it, and we wish to avoid what is evil and yet we perform it. How much fear and worry are created through the varied conflicts and repressions. How often do we suffer through our unsatisfactory performances.

DELIVERANCE FROM HARMFUL HABITS

" DON'T drink anything but ordinary water ! "
" Smoke fewer cigarettes daily ! " This is
good advice from a famous doctor. But,
unfortunately, it is not everyone who prizes
this advice who is in a position to follow it.
He wants to act accordingly, but he cannot.
It is extraordinary ! The harder he tries, the
more fast he becomes caught in the net of bad
habit. It is the same as when we diet to reduce
superfluous flesh, and try to subjugate our
habit of eating plentifully. The final result is
that after a certain time we find ourselves
exceeding our usual amount. The only reliable
way to lay aside all bad habits is to uproot the
DESIRE which leads to it, and to replace it by a
useful habit. Whoever takes this road will
not only be freed and feel benefited thereby,
but will be unable to understand how he could
have been so enslaved, and will ask himself :
" How is it possible that I was once the victim
of this bad habit ? " whether it was a question

of drinking, smoking, stammering, blushing or twitching eyelids. Practice has shown that a record made to a general formula cannot guarantee success, if a subject should give way to drink because he is unlucky in love or for some other reason, but a special formula will succeed. Therefore, in each case, an individual mind-power record must be made, which is adapted not only to the person's character but to the special circumstances.

INCREASE OF PERSONAL EFFICIENCY

IF we imagine human life in the form of a curve, we can from the biological point of view verify the fact that this curve from youth upwards to forty years of age rises gradually, and then drops. It is now our task by the right influence to keep this curve at its highest point, so that we are able to work until a great age with undiminished vigour and efficiency. Increase of personal efficiency is to be attained by removing various repressions, as well as discord in love, marriage and friendship. We must not allow ourselves to be crippled by fate and in every situation we must be guided by the conviction that our destiny is in our own hands. There are no bad situations. There are only false and bad reactions. No matter in what situation we find ourselves, to-morrow we will do better, and develop a superiority complex in ourselves, and every day expect greater success. The present-day victims of unemployment have the greatest need of psychic help. To give these people new courage to face life and new confidence is one of the chief aims of psychophony. When it is a question of personal increase of efficiency, a good result is dependent on the correct deciphering of the psychic hieroglyphs of the human soul, whether it is a matter of personal or distant diagnosis. The latter is arrived at, not only through the personal answering of the psychic test on the part of the subject, but also through the intuition of the psychologist, because it is only on this basis that the individual record can be correctly manufactured and with it complete success achieved.

RELEASING AND DEVELOPMENT
OF TALENTS

IN our souls lie thousands of possibilities, of which we can make no conscious picture. They slumber in the depths of our unconscious minds and may be likened to the Sleeping Princess in *The Arabian Nights*. In earlier years the hypnotic or trance condition was used to release these talents. This condition revealed the talents in the same manner as a volcanic mountain is lit up by its eruption.

It is a long time since Mr. James Braid, the Manchester surgeon, through the medium of hypnotism, enabled an actress to take the part of a fellow artiste, who had become indisposed, although she had only heard the part once, and to play it in such a manner that she not only showed herself a brilliant performer but did not omit one word of the part.

In Munich in 1904, under the presidency of the well-known psychiatrist, Dr. Schrenk-Notzing, the presentation of the dream-dancer, Magdalene, took place. She was capable of

77

dancing only when under the influence of hypnosis, and in a normal condition had no mastery of this art.

After psychic influence had reached a stage in its development when suggestion when in a waking condition began to usurp the place hitherto held by hypnosis, due to the belief that the same results could be achieved by suggestion, it is not surprising that we succeeded in producing the same results in this direction with mind-power records. Our first attempts took place in Stockholm, where, under the influence of the mind-power records, young people from the audience, without any preparation whatsoever, danced, improvised and sang, as if they were recognized artistes. In order to avoid any misunderstanding, it must here be emphasized that it is impossible to produce genius in this way, but only through the removal of psychic repressions, such as lack of self-confidence, nervousness at appearing in public to set free talent, which is already in existence, although it may happen never to have been detected. It is impossible to make a great artiste of someone who has no innate talent, but it is possible to assist a real artiste to a hundred per cent execution by freeing him from psychic repressions. One cannot make someone play the piano who has not already acquired technique by years of practice, but one can enhance his execution once this technique has been acquired. What is the most perfect technique without an execution which is spiritually moving ? It is like a flower without scent. By means of the mind-power records, however, it is possible to strengthen emotion and to improve the capacity for expression, so that it seems as if the performer had really experienced everything.

You have all heard of stage fright, the greatest dread of all artistes and public speakers. Let us suppose that one of us must suddenly appear on the stage before a large audience, and play the part of some great personality. At the same moment in which we must respond to the emergency, we feel our heart beginning to beat quickly, our hands shake, and we are seized with the feeling that we shall be laughed at. It is as if our talent had become paralysed, and in the instant in which we stand before the audience we are like a motor, some of whose cylinders have suddenly ceased to function. What actually has happened ? Self-criticism and harmful auto-suggestion have suppressed our artistic gifts, and the psychic energy has dispersed in stage fright. All logical exhortations in such a case are useless. Only through the mechanical influence of the subconscious mind can confidence in the face of a public appearance be re-won, and the repressed energy set free, then to be discharged in the form of a magnificent artistic performance. It would be wasted labour, however, to manufacture a pattern " talent record " for such a purpose. For people who do not believe in their capacity it is necessary to eliminate all the details of their stage fright and repressions so that it is then possible to make a special record, which will be efficacious because it is specially adapted to their particular character and case. Even the characteristic speech of the subject must be used in the suggested formula. Therefore, in distant treatment, not only must the psychophonic test be filled in by the student entirely by himself, but in it he should make use of his characteristic speech and manner of expressing himself. It must also be emphasized in connection with the ensuing results that everything here also runs an individual course. In some cases the best results show themselves within a few days. In other cases the effect of the suggestion is absent for weeks, to appear suddenly at a later date.

PSYCHOPHONY IN THE FILM
STUDIO

THE film is such an important feature of the life of to-day, that I feel I must write a few lines on the use of psychophony in the film studio.

There is no art which is so completely dependent on the form of the expressions of the artistes.

Have we ever thought of what exactly takes place when scenes are being shot in a film studio ? The arrival early in the morning, dressing and undressing in more or less cold dressing-rooms and the noise and hubbub. *What an atmosphere is that of the studio !* Here there is no feeling for dignity, and none of the respect which enforces silence when any other artistic performance is taking place. In the shooting of a film, everything is subordinated to machinery, to the importance of cameramen, electricians, etc. And in this atmosphere artistes are expected to express the most intense and realistic emotions ! What enormous psychic strength is necessary for the artistes to concentrate to such an extent that they are unaffected by their surroundings.

Psychophony is a wonderful aid to enable them to arrive at a state of detachment from their material surroundings.

More than that, psychophony can have a great influence on the art of cinematography. I assert that a great film is one in which the artistes interpret emotions and sentiments with such clearness that the audience perceives and understands them as soon as it sees the faces on the screen.

A film actor, writing about his art, says that all facial expressions which do not correspond to a definite thought are not sufficiently precise to make comprehensible to the audience, in a given moment, the state of mind of the person represented. That is as good as to say, that it is necessary for a film actor to banish from his mind all critical and irrelevant thoughts ; in other words, he must suggest, and the whole art of the cinema is to understand and suggest the part one is playing.

Those sentiments which the actor is to portray must be reflected on the screen with perfect clarity and definition. What a wonderful aid the psychophonic record is in helping the artiste by means of suggestion to overcome difficulties in the way of his full expression of his talent.

I can imagine what support could be given by a stimulating and confidence-inspiring voice, when one was speaking a language with which one was not at home, or using a diction with which one was not familiar.

ENHANCING SPIRITUAL GIFTS

SPECIAL mind-power records can succeed in attuning the individual or medium to a certain frame of mind, in which the subconscious mind is stimulated, in a way in which the individual or medium alone could not succeed in doing.

I should like here to quote a famous medium, Ossowiecki, who is a personal friend of mine. He writes in his book entitled *The Realm of My Spirit* as follows :

" The fear that the experiment may fail affects my psyche negatively."

Referring to his gift he says :

" From inner experience I know that I can see far back into the past. By making a great effort I can see the world with my spiritual eye, but in order to arrive at the conditions necessary for enabling me to do this *I must disconnect and completely shut out my conscious mind, so that my own ego is put aside.*"

It is just this disconnecting of the conscious mind which is one of the most difficult tasks, and in which even the best medium may fail if unaided. The necessary aid is given by psychophony.

In this connection, the best example that can be given is that of the clairvoyante, Sabira, a medium belonging to an aristocratic Tartar family. I have performed thousands of experiments with her with the greatest success, and she is now able at any moment to call up her powers of clairvoyance to such a degree of intensity that she is able to diagnose any illness from which a person may be suffering, and this diagnosis is confirmed by doctors in every single case.

She was, of course, born with unusual gifts in this direction, but until she met me she had been unable to develop them fully, and my methods enabled her to cultivate the power of disconnecting her conscious mind, leaving her free to develop her gifts to perfection.

YOUTH AND BEAUTY FROM
INWARDS OUTWARDS

FURTHER, the mind-power records make it possible to win back youth and develop beauty in quite a new way, by setting the inner powers of the subconscious mind working for this aim. Is it not comprehensible that more is to be achieved by this means than Steinach and Voronoff have achieved, working on the physical side, by strengthening the glands through purely physical means, when we are fully aware of the extraordinary effect which suggestion can have on the glandular functions, and that, therefore, psychophonic suggestion leads to psychic rejuvenation, so that the person who has received treatment will once more see life from the fresh and enthusiastic view-point of youth, and not only the body, but also the soul will have become young ? We can all call to mind certain well-known actresses, who are no longer young in years, yet not only appear young on the stage, but *are* young in private life. This is only to be explained by the force of suggestion, in that they have played youthful roles on the stage until, in identifying themselves with the character they are impersonating, they have also identified themselves with the youth of these persons, and this has brought about their own rejuvenation.

In the *Daily Express* of 4th June, 1935, there appeared an article under the title of " The Chance of Long Life is Better. Six and a Half Years up on 1910." In this article it is stated that Sir Frank Smith, Secretary of the Department of Scientific and Industrial Research, said that :

" But just as engineers give us results in terms of increase of a motor tyre or modern boiler, so can those who have made progress in the King's reign in the fight against suffering and disease point proudly to a figure of six and a half years for the average increase in the expectancy of life during the last twenty-five years.

" The increase is not due to taking better care of ourselves. It is the result of better water supplies, better hygiene and increased skill in surgery."

Is it not obvious that, if to the above-mentioned achievements which result in longer life we add mental training by means of psychophony, the chances of, not only a longer life, but also longer youth, are immeasurably increased ?

At the time of Alexander Dumas a woman of thirty was considered to have passed the stage of her youth. To-day there is many a woman of forty who can truthfully claim to be still young, and it is significant that the age at which women underwent what is commonly called the change of life has been transferred in the course of the last thirty or forty years from about forty to forty-eight.

These changes have taken place in spite of the fact that the mental strain and stress of modern life is far greater than ever before. There is no doubt that, once psychophonic treatment has counterbalanced this strain, the prolongation of life and youth to which we have referred may be counted, not in years, but in decades.

In fact, the process of rejuvenation is based on the same law as the shaping and growth of a child, and cells in the tissues of an octogenarian build and rebuild in the same manner as those in the tissues of a new-born baby. The difference, therefore, lies in erroneous thinking, which identifies the

(Left)

A PHASE IN THE MAKING
OF
A MIND-POWER RECORD

(Centre)
TESTING THE
PSYCHIC
POWER OF A
MIND-POWER
RECORD

(Right)

INCREASE OF PHYSICAL STRENGTH
THROUGH MIND-POWER RECORDS

The increase is measured by a dynamometer.

physical appearance with the number of years lived, and so prevents the cells from showing the youth which they are in reality creating.

Can you not picture to yourself what good results would accrue for anyone at a critical age who received the following psychophonic suggestion daily :

‘ My subconscious mind obeys my commands. It is rejuvenating my arteries, revitalizing my blood, rejuvenating me entirely, strengthening the function of my glands, and increasing my psychic and physical vitality. It is increasing the functioning of my tissues and muscles. Day and night it works more and more to express in my body the perfect image of my real self which God created. I can remain young, capable and slim for ever. Rejuvenation, harmony and beauty are manifesting now.”

Do you not believe that, if these ideas are composed in a suitable suggestive form and the person concerned plays them on a special mind-power record every night before going to sleep, so that all night long the subconscious mind is working on these lines, they will in time become reality ? Why not, when we all know how harmful auto-suggestion works on certain women who grow prematurely old, merely through the fear of age, which prompts them, as soon as they wake in the morning, to go to their mirrors and search anxiously for wrinkles, which their very anxiety and pre-occupation with this suggestion produce, so that the physical ravages wrought in their faces by their inner discord and psychic conflicts become apparent ?

THE USE OF PSYCHOPHONY IN CHILD WELFARE

IT is appropriate here to say a few words about the use of psychophony in dealing with backward or defective children. It is a matter of moral orthopædy, applied to children who suffer from any defect of character or bad habit, such as lying, nail-biting, wetting the bed, etc., or to children who are generally refractory. It is psychophony's useful mission to correct the faults in the minds of these children, and develop all their good potentialities.

The child's soul may well be compared to a piece of wax, as it is so remarkable and susceptible to the suggestions which reach and impress it by means of the records just before the child falls asleep, and which work all through the night in its subconscious mind for its benefit.

Of first importance, of course, is the

special individual record, which is adapted exactly to the child's individuality while the general records serve to cultivate will-power, confidence, courage, concentration and memory.

PSYCHOPHONY AND MEDICAL
TREATMENT

THE science of modern pathology has established definitely that the principal cause of such psycho-neurotic phenomena as cardiac neurosis, nervous dyspepsia, psychic impotence, etc., is to be sought, not in physical factors, but in the disturbing element in the patient's mind and in his morbid thoughts.

Of course, you have heard of the ridiculous but pathetic cases of people who are unable to walk through a certain place. Is it a physical disability which produces these nervous symptoms ? It is not.

Their physical condition enables them to walk or talk perfectly well ; it is only their subconscious mind which produces apprehensions which make them as impotent to proceed as if they were paralysed.

In order to combat these phenomena, it is only natural to make use of the same weapons as those used by the adversary, and so modern psychotherapy makes use of psycho-analysis

and auto-suggestion in attempting to overcome neurasthenia, hysteria and what is now
called psychasthenia.

During the Great War marvellous results
were obtained by means of this treatment in
cases of psychic aphonia and functional
paralysis.

This is why all doctors who have had
occasion to make use of the new psychotherapy are united in declaring that psycho-
analysis and auto-suggestion are capable of
removing all psycho-neuroses.

But others go further and state that auto-
suggestion is equally capable of combating
organic disease.

Dr. Bonjour quotes the case of a wart which
was very rapidly cured by auto-suggestion.
The doctor asserts that he has obtained
positive results from using auto-suggestion
for diabetics. Not only was their general
condition improved, but the quantity of sugar
dropped from seventy-nine to twenty-five
grammes.

Finally, Dr. Charles Beaudouin declared
that he had reduced an ulcer solely by means
of auto-suggestion. What is the significance
of all this ?

We are in the presence of scientific facts,

but we have within us forces the strength of which we are unable even to guess at.

Dr. Jolowicz, of Berlin University, speaks of the powerful psychic regenerative forces which are latent in us. He states that in us exist creative and reconstructive forces which serve to combat those agents which produce disease. In everyone's system there is a natural inclination towards harmony, and balance of the various functions rules. The reconstructive powers in our system function automatically without the aid of our will, and we can mobilize them by means of our inner confidence and use them for curing our ills.

And if we reflect, what is vaccination if it is not the creation in our organism of beneficial anti-toxins, which defends our system from the attacks of disease, and arouses all our defensive forces to combat ?

In the same way a surgeon uses stitching to help to heal the wound he has suddenly made, and to encourage the regrowth of the tissues, and prevent our system from suffering more than is necessary.

To resume, we see that a cure can take place inwardly, but we have not yet complete knowledge of how it is effected, or of exactly what exterior elements contribute towards it.

The more you recall what I said at the beginning of this book, the more convinced you will be that modern science is right in declaring that in each illness at least 50 per cent of the cause may be attributed to psychic factors.

Now I come to psychophony. Without going into long explanations, I will say that it serves to reduce this 50 per cent of unfavourable psychic element, and so facilitate amelioration of the case.

It can also mobilize in our system all the curative forces which have been lying there unused but only require the correct instigation to be set in motion for our benefit.

We must picture this as the mobilization of an army, which is called to the colours by means of mechanical suggestion.

However, it would be both undesirable and against psychophonic principles to omit ordinary medical treatment in a case of organic disease. In fact, psychophony signifies an enrichment of therapy, and in the case of serious organic disease serves as an aid to the doctor who is treating the case, and offers him a new weapon in combating disease.

We will now answer several questions which are often put to us.

1. How do the records themselves have an effect without the suggestionist?

Experience has taught that reason, criticism and will-power prevent the health suggestion from penetrating the subconscious mind. By obtaining the required conditions, that is by a coloured light, by relaxing and by frequent repetitions of the health suggestion, we are enabled to set the subconscious mind in motion so that we can realize our wishes.

One can understand that, in this way, the mind-power records, having procured relaxation and set the subconscious mind in motion through a sufficient number of repetitions, have the best possible results.

With this technique, the person concerned has no need to trouble himself with the progress resulting from the treatment, as the results are produced automatically.

2. Why does the mind-power record achieve good results?

In using the radio you will remember that, when you switch on the apparatus, for example, to hear certain music, that music was already present in the ether, and it becomes audible when you connect with the required wave-

G

length. The same thing takes place with psychophony. Our subconscious mind possesses forces, which only require to be set in motion in order to obtain the necessary good results. Just in the same way in which we make use of the radio in order to obtain the music we want, so must we use psychophony to link up our subconscious mind with the mind of the suggestionist in order that we may have it working for our benefit.

3. DOES THE DAILY REPETITION OF THE RECORDS DULL THEIR EFFECT ?

When first using the records we are far too conscious of and attentive to the records, whereas later we give them ever-diminishing attention, so that the suggestions penetrate more easily into our subconscious minds. The effect increases with every repetition.

4. WHY IS IT NOT POSSIBLE VERY OFTEN TO OBTAIN GOOD RESULTS WITH ONE'S OWN WILL-POWER ?

Coué has already discovered that there is opposition between will-power and the subconscious mind, and that through forcing will-power we often obtain adverse results. It is well known that the more a person exerts

his will-power to make himself fall asleep, the
less likely he is to induce that state. Dr.
Alexander Cannon has put this very simply in
another way. The conscious mind likes to
command the individual. When it detects
the subconscious mind gaining control, the
conscious mind fights for its life, and negativism or extreme stubbornness results until
the battle is fought and won and the subconscious mind reigns supreme in power
with the conscious mind in subordination.
The record mechanically sets our subconscious mind in harmonic rhythmic motion,
and sleep and peace of mind automatically
ensue.

5. IS IT NECESSARY FOR THE SUGGESTIONIST
TO GIVE THE SUGGESTIONS PERSONALLY?

The personal power of the suggestionist is
transferred to the record, so that we receive
the same vibrations as if the suggestionist himself were speaking. One advantage must not
be forgotten. For every student a special
record will be made, which will be adapted to
his particular character and temperament, and
will be in a style and phrasing with which he
is most familiar. In this way the record has
an individual and personal effect.

6. WHAT IS THE DIFFERENCE BETWEEN HYPNOSIS AND THE MIND-POWER RECORDS?

In some cases hypnosis calls up unconscious opposition in the patient because he feels uncomfortable at the thought of being influenced by a stranger, whereas the mind-power record is only mechanical hetero-suggestion, which becomes auto-suggestion, and arouses no opposition in the patient, and he is able to repeat them as often as he needs.

7. WHAT IS THE RELATION BETWEEN THE SUBCONSCIOUS MIND AND AUTO-SUGGESTION?

The subconscious mind rules all sympathetic and unconscious functions. Normal heart action depends on it ; it regulates the secretion of the glands, the circulation of the blood, breathing and digestion. At its instigation we draw away our fingers from a burning object before we have seen it. The subconscious mind calls forth an unconscious reaction to guard us from a danger before we have become aware of it. This subconscious mind is far more powerful than our conscious will. In us is a force which works like the ship's engines under the decks, and, like the ship's passengers, we are only aware of its existence through seeing the results of its working.

With suggestive activity we can only be sure of one thing, and it is that the subconscious mind can be set in motion by a vivid representation, and every result of this is evoked in like manner to the releasing of various articles from an automatic machine by the insertion of coins.

In the subconscious mind lie unused immeasurable forces, which can, by means of the mind-power records, be set in motion for our benefit.

8. DO YOU NOT BELIEVE THAT THE SUBCONSCIOUS MIND WORKS FOR YOU?

Then pay attention to the following. Here is an example from one of the many everyday incidents you experience without realizing the significance behind it.

Suppose that, immediately before falling asleep, you make up your mind to awaken at a certain time in the morning. You will find that you succeed in doing so. Have you ever thought there was something wonderful in this? There is, in fact, nothing extraordinary about it, as it is only the result of the working of your subconscious mind, which in this case has proved itself your helpmate.

In just the same way the subconscious mind can carry out the commands given by the mind-power records. Psychophony means the training of your subconscious mind in the service of your health, success and happiness.

FACTS SPEAK FOR THEMSELVES

IN October, 1931, I was invited by the committee of the International Congresses for Psychotherapy and Practical Psychology to be present at the Congress in Paris, and on the 3rd October I gave a demonstration of my methods in the Science Auditorium, when they aroused great interest and appreciation.

Since then Radwan Institutes have been founded in Stockholm, Oslo, Berlin, Amsterdam and other cities, and people from all classes and in all positions in life, bank employees and directors, teachers, university students, engineers, factory foremen, journalists, business men, artists and housewives have received psychophonic treatment in their homes, either after consultation at the institutes, or, if they lived at too great a distance, by correspondence.

To these Continental institutes a Radwan Institute has now been added in London, and the organization of branch institutes in other cities of Great Britain and the Empire is under consideration.

Many of those who have been treated by psychophony have written describing the great benefit they had derived. These letters are at the disposal of bona fide inquirers at the Radwan Institute, Ltd., London.

In the following will be found a list of typical cases which have been cured by the Radwan method, many of them after all other treatments had failed. Where necessary, details are extracted from the records.

1. *Stage Fright.* The obsession of fear from which this singer suffered, resulted in hoarseness and even loss of voice, whenever he was to appear in public. (Completely recovered.)

2. *Mental and physical tiredness.* The patient could no longer walk upright, and could only move at a slow pace. Self-confidence had vanished almost entirely. (Completely recovered.)

3. *Fear.* The patient suffered from "an indescribable feeling of fear when in the street." He was afraid that "a tile from a

roof might fall on his head" and this made him afraid to go out. (Completely recovered.)

4. *Fear.* (*a*) An otherwise healthy man, aged about forty, was obsessed by the fear that he was unable to cross a street or square. He felt that his legs became weak, that he grew faint, and the result was that he would be unable to make even a single step. This obsession occurred regularly and at times became so strong that if he had, by a great effort of will, set out to cross the street, he dropped to the ground in the middle of the road, and was unable to rise again. From the time when the first attack occurred he was in constant fear of a recurrence, and consequently these attacks did actually become regular.

When the patient consulted the Institute he had not dared to leave his house for several years. After a few weeks' treatment by the psychophonic method this patient was entirely cured.

(*b*) Another case refers to a young man at the end of his twenties. He was of athletic build with a very fine muscular development. He practised many sports, particularly the lifting of exceptionally heavy weights. He was in a perfectly healthy condition. When he

called at the Institute he stated that for many
years the thought had very frequently occurred
to him that he was incapable of writing. This
obsession was so intense that it deprived him
of the strength required to hold a pen, so that
he was unable to write even his signature.
Gradually this condition became permanent.
In consequence of this his career had suffered
very much, and gradually he had lost all
confidence in himself and all hope of recovery.
He had tried various cures and had been
under medical treatment but without obtaining
any improvement in his condition. When
he came to the Institute his mental condition
was one of utter despair and despondency,
bordering on insanity. About two months'
treatment by psychophony were sufficient to
remove his trouble entirely and permanently.

(c) A medical practitioner submitted the
following case to the Institute. His young
wife, who had been a very well-known and
active Society woman and possessed a very
striking appearance and perfect health, had
suddenly undergone a very distressing change
for the worse in consequence of a dream.
She had dreamt that she had lost her way and,
wandering at random through the country-side,
had found herself suddenly at the gate of a

churchyard. Here she was met by a mysterious apparition who led her to a recently
made grave, at the head of which was a tablet
with an inscription. When she read this
inscription she was horrified to find that it
consisted of her name and surname and the
date of her death, about three months ahead
of the date on which the dream occurred. At
this stage she awoke from her nightmare in
an almost hysterical condition. From that
moment onwards her attitude to life changed
entirely. She ceased her social activities and
refused to see anyone except her husband and
one or two intimate friends. She became
despondent and indifferent to everything.
When urged to go out and return to her old
mode of living, she replied always by the same
answer : " Why should I, when I am to die
in a few months ? " After a few weeks of
psychophonic treatment this young woman
became again entirely normal and regained
her joy in living. She was then utterly unable
to understand why this dream should have
ever influenced her mind.

(d) A university student, although quite
healthy, was unable to control his thoughts
when he had to ascend stairs. On such
occasions the first symptom which occurred

was that he felt compelled to count the steps. The next feeling was that he was possessed by an evil spirit and gradually would go mad. His heart would begin to beat very rapidly and irregularly, he felt giddy and grew pale. This case required psychophonic treatment during a long period, but finally the patient was entirely cured.

5. *Excessive smoking.* Experience has shown that the cases which respond most readily to psychophonic treatment are those relating to bad habits, such as gambling, excessive smoking, drinking and drug habits. The following is a typical example. An elderly business man had gradually become a very heavy cigarette smoker, his daily average being eighty to a hundred cigarettes. As he was suffering from kidney trouble his medical adviser had forbidden him to smoke. The patient had tried all kinds of cures and had also applied his willpower to the problem but had been entirely unable to rid himself of this bad habit. As soon as his mind was occupied with business problems or with any other engrossing thoughts he would smoke one cigarette after the other quite unconsciously. When he consulted me I instructed him to ignore his bad habit

altogether, and not to give any thought to his desire to rid himself of it. All he was advised to do was to play a specially prepared psychophonic record every night before going to sleep. After three weeks of this treatment he reported that he had lost all desire to smoke and that he did not miss his cigarettes in the least. Later reports were to the effect that the cure had been permanent.

6. *Nervous digestive troubles.* Another interesting case is that of a man who gambled very heavily on the Stock Exchange. When the market became unfavourable to his operations he was immediately seized by acute nervous stomachic and intestinal trouble. This at last reached a point where his friends and acquaintances knew from his state of health whenever he had losses. During the first weeks of treatment by psychophony there was no result whatsoever, and I discovered that this was due to the fact that he was constantly watching himself to discover whether there was any improvement. This intensive preoccupation of his mind counteracted the effect of the records. I explained this to him, and asked him to adopt an entirely passive attitude of mind. *A few days'* treat-

ment then brought about an improvement and after two weeks he was entirely cured.

7. *Harmony in marriage.* A prominent business man told me that he was quarrelling frequently with his wife, and that these quarrels upset him to such a degree that he was unable to concentrate his mind on his business, with consequent serious losses. I found that on the slightest provocation coming from his wife his reaction was very violent and that this provoked his wife to increased counter-attacks. This patient was given a special record which caused him to remain indifferent to any criticisms, reproaches and attacks, meeting them good-humouredly, calmly and smilingly. One month's treatment removed not only the previously existing distressing effects, but his wife also gradually desisted from her attacks, so that complete harmony was restored.

8. *Despondency.* An unemployed " blackcoated worker " had become so despondent and depressed that he had given up trying to find employment. A short period of treatment by psychophonic records restored his willpower and hope, with the result that he

obtained a new and better post, and was able to do his work with greater energy than ever before.

9. *Nervous breakdown.* After a long illness which weakened his whole system, this patient had to undergo three operations, one of which was very serious. Circumstances prevented him from taking a good holiday after the operations and forced him to go back to work before he had regained his normal strength. The result was that he became more and more nervous and broken in health. Nerve pains, insomnia and acute irritability occurred more and more frequently. At this stage he began psychophonic treatment. After a few months the improvement was already remarkable. The pains and insomnia disappeared, he became calmer and more certain of himself. His carriage and bearing improved so that his friends immediately noticed the change. His output of work increased and he felt joy and interest in life.

10. *Worry on sexual matters.* This patient worried over sexual matters to such an extent that he lost interest in everything. Loss of appetite resulted in loss of weight. He would

lie awake most of the night worrying over sexual matters. Finally he was unable to carry on his work.

Doctors prescribed sleeping draughts, but in spite of these his condition became worse and his thoughts became more and more disconnected.

Soon after beginning the psychophonic treatment an improvement set in. After a few weeks the patient was able to control himself. Within three or four minutes of playing the evening records he would fall asleep and sleep peacefully the whole night through. His weight gradually returned to normal. His worry over sexual matters had entirely disappeared.

11. *Paralysis.* This young patient had been completely paralysed for years and incapable of making any movement. According to the latest report (14th May, 1935), written by his brother, he " showed decided improvement, raising himself from the armchair by himself and attempting to walk without support from the chair to the sofa. In this attitude he manages to make about eight to ten steps. He has invariably done the same thing every day after the relaxation

INSOMNIA IS CURED BY A SPECIAL MIND-POWER RECORD

record, until the present day. During our festivals (Jubilee) he sat up at table in an arm-chair propped up with cushions and showed no signs of exhaustion. His face looks quite cheerful and healthy. My brother tells me he feels that the strengthening of his will-power, noted in my last report, is still being maintained."

12. *Dementia præcox.* (*a*) This case had been diagnosed by doctors as *dementia præcox* and treated for a number of years without any improvement being obtained. The patient was then treated by the Radwan system, and after a few weeks wrote the following letter to the Institute :

" *2nd April,* 1935.

Each day I have had the treatment at home I have gained confidence, and have really benefited by all that has been done for me. I feel much more self-confident and happy, and have hope of making a success of my future and have full control of myself. I still hear voices but am no longer troubled about it, as I feel in some cases they wish to help me and if possible guide me. Anything that puzzles me I can put out of my mind, my

H

resistance to anything I do not wish to notice is stronger, and so I feel I have benefited greatly and have gained fresh courage.

O. M. J."

(b) The following letter was received from the mother of another patient suffering from the same complaint :

" 29th March, 1935.

Margaret is quite a different being to-day, most extraordinarily better, so I write on behalf of my husband and myself to thank you for the amazing miracle that has been performed. The rest of her life would have been misery without what you have achieved for her, and we should have been worn-out wrecks. Her appearance has improved considerably, and she has lost the hunted, staring look she had. She is as normal as she could be expected to be after the last three years, and perhaps the remainder can be cleared up.

M. M."

13. *Epilepsy*. The patient, who lives several hundred miles from London, was unable to come to the Institute because he had at least one, and sometimes more than one, fit per day. This condition had lasted for years and

all methods of treatment had failed to bring about any improvement. His wife reported that "he was slipping away very rapidly." After four weeks' psychophonic treatment the intervals between the attacks began to increase, and after three months the patient seemed to be cured permanently. At the time of writing he had not had an attack for five weeks. He is nevertheless continuing to use the records.

The cases which give the best proof are those where all other methods have failed, and especially the cases of sceptics and critically inclined persons, and of those in whom the person of a hypnotist arouses strong unconscious opposition. In all these cases psychophony is the only efficacious medium. Although psychophony is hetero-suggestion, it is applied by means of the records, and so does not call up the unconscious resistance which is often aroused by the personal element in hypnotic treatment.

The important feature is that it does not work through the conscious mind but directly through the subconscious mind, and for this reason the patient does not need to trouble himself about the process or to assist it in any way. On the contrary, unlike psycho-analysis and other auto-suggestion methods (Couéism), in psychophony the less the patient troubles himself about the process, the more easily are the inner healing forces automatically set in motion, and the desired results arrived at.

Here follow examples :

1. *Stage fright.* A very well-known pianist, Mr. S., living in London, had suffered for years from very bad stage fright. Finally this increased to such an extent that he felt convinced that, as soon as he commenced to play in public, his hands would become like ice. This harmful auto-suggestion appeared with such intensity that his hands not only felt like ice, but actually became blue. An eight weeks' treatment by the psychophonic system with general and special records achieved 100 per cent results, and the artiste is now able to appear with the greatest success.

2. *Stammering.* A very gifted young man, Mr. M., was unable to advance in his business career owing to a stammer, from which he had suffered from childhood. His family was worried and his father sent him to well-known specialists, from whom he received

treatment for many years, but without any result.

The psychophonic treatment which he underwent only lasted four months before a permanent cure was effected. During the first weeks of the treatment, he was able one week to speak much better, and then again another week his speech would be much worse again. Finally the individual special record won the victory, so that now, after four months, he speaks like a normal person, has won back his confidence, and is progressing in his career.

3. *Utter despondency.* A well-known leader of industry, a cool and calculating business man, Mr. H., was so badly affected by an unhappy love affair that he became like a living corpse. For a whole year he was unable to direct his business, and became extremely emaciated. After a year of unsuccessful treatment by the best specialists on the Continent, he came to me in 1934. His state almost bordered on insanity. He suffered from the obsession that he must think of a girl for the rest of his life, although he himself had abused her as a selfish, heartless, worthless creature. His power of concentration had become so weak that he was forced to repeat a word many

times over before he could fix it in his memory.

After three months' treatment with psychophony he obtained a 100 per cent cure, and his mental capacity was so increased that he was able to carry out remarkable business transactions. His acquaintances could scarcely recognize him as the same man.

When, later, he heard news of the girl (who had become a film star) he was able to receive it with complete indifference, as if it related to a stranger.

4. *Hereditary neurasthenia.* (*a*) A merchant, Mr. H., fifty-six years of age, living in Hamburg, suffered from hereditary neurasthenia. His mother had had almost the same symptoms. For twenty-four years he went from one nursing home to another for treatment.

The chief symptoms were that he was easily exhausted, and suffered from depression and a feeling of inferiority. In 1902 signs of insomnia appeared and gradually became permanent. For years he had to make use of sleeping draughts.

He went to bed at about ten o'clock, and fell asleep at about midnight. For ten years he took Adalin tablets. He always awakened of his own accord at 2.30 a.m. Then followed three hours of sound sleep, after which he suffered from nightmares. A few minutes' sleep was followed by periods of wakefulness. At the first noise in the morning he was seized with the dreaded thought : " Now I will be unable to sleep any more." He had an ever-present fear that sooner or later someone in an adjoining room would make a noise.

Apart from the fear of noise, he was tormented by the fear of light, and, before falling asleep, by various anxieties, such as business worries and other obsessions, which he was unable to banish. The worst feature was that after sleeping badly he believed himself incapable of working, and was restless and unable to relax during the whole day.

In the hope of getting some sleep at midday he used to bandage his eyes. When he tried to sleep after his lunch he became concerned regarding the process of digestion and went to the lavatory several times, because he suffered from the obsession that while something remained unevacuated he could not sleep.

He was treated by a well-known psychotherapist in Baden-Baden, who every day attempted to place him in a half-sleep, but without result. All suggestions failed. Weeks of auto-suggestion methods and formulæ had no effect. Other psychotherapists declared that he possessed too much resistance. He was later treated according to psycho-analytical methods for many weeks. In the presence of the doctor he had to look at the wall for a certain time, during which he had to utter aloud every thought which passed through his mind. This also failed to produce any result.

He was also treated by a hypnotist without any success.

After four weeks of psychophonic treatment, Mr. H. was able to sleep without the aid of narcotics, although not without interruption. After two weeks' treatment with the special record he was no longer affected by insomnia and felt fresh, strong and capable for work.

After a few months he informed me that he was able to sleep soundly and peacefully the whole night through, and that after his midday sleep he awakened full of renewed energy and vitality.

(b) Dr. A. D., thirty-three years of age, had suffered from neurasthenia since childhood. His mother was highly nervous, and, among other fears, had that of being unable to swallow. His father, a cashier, had never permitted soiled money to be placed on the table. At a later stage the patient had to consult an oculist and was found to be suffering from trachoma. For this reason the father continuously admonished the child : " Keep your hands away from your eyes, and wash your hands ! "

As a small child he also expressed a feeling of disgust when his sister kissed him, probably for the reason that her hands were damp. When he was fifteen, he had boils, from which he suffered until he was twenty-five. At the age of twenty-two he was once advised by the family doctor to keep his clothes clean and especially his collars. All this developed in him a mania for perpetual washing himself and cleaning everything with which he came into contact.

He suffered from acute disgust and fears, especially in regard to skin diseases. He was unable to touch anyone if he saw that the person was suffering from any kind of rash. If circumstances compelled him to be near such a person he was convinced that the bacilli had been transferred to him. He felt compelled to go and wash himself at once.

The mere sight of anyone suffering from eczema made him go pale, and he always

carried with him alcohol, soap and brushes, so
that he could cleanse himself after even indirect contact with the person concerned.
When he happened to see anyone with a
flushed face in a restaurant, and observed that
they were both served by the same waiter, he
was struck with the thought that the waiter
probably had touched his glass, and at once
felt repulsion and the desire to clean his glass.
His worst difficulty was with soiled money,
so that as soon as he had touched it he felt
compelled to wash his hands. Not only that,
he even had to wash the money itself, and if
his wife had touched it he insisted that she
also should wash herself thoroughly. It was
the same with soiled documents. There was,
however, one exception. When he wore his
office suit, which naturally came into contact
with papers handled by all kinds of people,
he was relieved to feel no necessity of cleansing
this suit, although if his hands even touched
it he was still impelled to wash them at once.
The same thing happened when he went to
the barber's. On such occasions he always
wore his office suit, as, in his opinion, the
wearing of any of his other clothes would have
necessitated their disinfection. When he had
guests whom he suspected of having touched

soiled money, or when colleagues were with him, who, in the course of their business, handled all kinds of documents, he must, after their departure, clean all the furniture and wash everything. This labour of cleansing often lasted the whole night. He even went so far as to disinfect with iodoform any flowers which happened to be in the room. On such occasions he also expected his wife and the other members of his family to wash themselves immediately. If, by a great effort of will, he suppressed the desire for cleansing, he was restless until he had performed it at some later date, often after several days had elapsed. When asked if he would not have been satisfied if the cleaning had been carried out by a servant instead of by himself, his answer was that he would not have trusted her to clean everything as thoroughly and minutely as he himself had done.

While on active service during the War he risked his life by leaving the trenches and running about in search of water, wherewith to cleanse himself after contact with his companions.

When his wife returned from any social engagement, he insisted that she should clean her clothes and wash herself thoroughly.

Generally he had not so much fear of infection as an æsthetic repulsion. Thus, for instance, in the presence of a case of typhus he felt no fear and did not even feel prompted to wash himself.

He was indeed aware that it was all nonsense, but, nevertheless, had no peace of mind until he felt cleansed again. For this purpose he kept in his house specially prepared towels. Thus, while he felt that he *must* disinfect himself, he was at the same time convinced that it did not help at all. Again, if he should come to hear of anything " unclean " that had happened weeks before, he would at once proceed to disinfect everything connected with it, regardless of the lapse of time.

He felt a particular repulsion for doctors and postmen, and it was sufficient for him to read or hear the word " blood poisoning " to call up all his complexes.

When he was twenty-eight he was treated by a psycho-analyst. For five weeks he went to him every day for an hour, because this doctor explained to him that he had arrived at the so-called black point. Later he was treated by psycho-analysis in a clinic, where he was questioned about his dreams. After these two treatments proved fruitless, he lost all faith in psycho-analysis. He also received treatment from a well-known specialist by means of hypnosis, but without any result. The same specialist had given him a page of suggestion formulæ on the Coué model to be repeated before going to sleep, but this also failed to produce any improvement.

Being very critical and inclined to negativism he was convinced that he was not a suitable subject for treatment by suggestion. For instance, when told : " You will be healthy," the thought at once occurred to him : " But you will not be healthy." Apart from this, he was possessed by doubts, and from childhood on was inclined to be moody. He also suffered from a lack of concentration.

Then he was given the psychophonic treatment of morning, afternoon and evening records, and of the special individual record, used immediately before his afternoon sleep.

His desire to cleanse and wash continually decreased until it reached a normal state.

These suggestions worked the whole time in his subconscious mind while he was sleeping in the afternoon, and the good results were arrived at automatically.

This patient was not a suitable subject for mechanical suggestion, and it was only through the frequent repetition of the individual record, which was used for a period of three months as an after-cure every day immediately before falling asleep, that practical success was achieved. After an interval of two weeks it was found necessary to use the general psycho-phonic influence for one month again, and in future he will probably have to visit a nursing home for a short period of about two weeks to repeat the treatment every two or three years in order to prevent any possible relapse.

RENEWAL OF THE HUMAN

HARMONY BETWEEN MIND AND BODY

THE reciprocal action between spirit, mind and body is known to everyone by everyday experience. Who does not know the physical consequences of the conception of fear ? The face becomes pale, the legs refuse to function and the heart begins to beat violently. Why ? Because every idea has a corresponding physical movement. It is sufficient, for instance, for a person to think intently of an action, to enable the experimenter to read that person's thoughts merely through touching his hand and feeling its involuntarily muscular movements. The action of the body and bodily changes on the spirit are witnessed by simple facts. A little coffee, alcohol or nicotine is sufficient to change a person's mood. Slight digestive trouble is enough to lower the efficiency of the greatest thinker. In the interests of our health, success and happiness we should give the reciprocal action between our bodies and spirits every thought. It would be just as wrong to attempt to help a person through physical remedies only as to attempt to help in some cases through psychic remedies only. In ordinary life it is possible to satisfy this principle of reciprocal action by a *positive conduct of life*, the aim of which is the renewal of vitality. The psychophonic life reform is the epitome of all endeavour directed towards increasing the value of the human personality by tending and furthering vitality, preserving youth in accordance with natural laws, and by giving life meaning through the development of intellect and character. We will here concern ourselves with the physical side of the task, and underline the great importance of *food reform*. In the care of health the present-day reformers set the greatest value *on prevention* and not on cure. *The illness of to-day is the consequence of the excesses of yesterday.* The best remedies will refuse to work if the defective diet is not corrected. The experiments of Osborn, Max Rubener, Liebig, Bertrand and Berg, have shown that besides albumen and fat, mineral substances and metals and even gold in the brain are important to life, to leave vitamins out of the question, and that the essential problem of food research is the finding of the right proportion of all these substances. It may also be said that every form of nourishment should be a remedy, that is, on the one side to provide the body with the necessary substance in which it is lacking, and on the other side to break up and eject the superfluous matter.

Even to the present day in spite of this scientific discovery civilized man is alien to a mode of life in full accordance with nature. We zealously overload our stomachs with meat, enjoy coffee or tea, and poison our system with tobacco and alcohol, and so prepare for ourselves a premature old age. In none of the creatures living in a state of nature do we find the serious chronic nervous and infectious diseases which make life a torment for man and this Earth a Hell. We who have at our service the conquests of professors and specialists, of doctors and chemists, and the products of laboratories and food factories as well as food tablets, live quite wrongly and reap, instead of health, strength and long life, sickness, weakness and early physical death. Even if we are not offered

I

every opportunity for making use of a perfect diet, and following an ideal mode of living, everyone can, at least, practise in moderation and follow the simple and practical rules contained in my practical course.

PHYSICAL AND MENTAL
HYGIENE

IN health economics the hypothesis on which we must base our efficiency is the correct harmony between the RECEPTION AND EXPENDITURE OF ENERGY. It follows, then, that it is advisable for those who wish to work well over a lengthy period to arrange for those conditions which allow them to keep their efficiency at a high peak permanently. Above all, fresh air to refresh the brain and to lighten exertion is necessary to produce good work. SLEEPING BY OPEN WINDOWS is recommended. Light walls, cheerful-coloured hangings lighten work and stimulate energy. Light and air! Experience shows that, to a great extent, we work with insufficient lighting. Scientific experiments have proved that for a workroom twelve feet square, a light of 300 candle-power is required. The temperature should be about 65 DEGREES FAHRENHEIT. As regards time, apart from individual dispositions, THE FORENOON IS THE MOST SUITABLE

TIME FOR STRENUOUS WORK, while the afternoon should be used for lighter tasks. Our relation to our surroundings is one of the most important chapters of spiritual and mental hygiene.

The presence of certain persons has a disturbing effect on our work. The psychic atmosphere in which we live and work is of the utmost significance. Therefore, we should confine our intercourse, as far as possible, to strong-willed, cheerful and competent people. We live in a time when man makes it his business at a great outlay to control the street traffic, which has grown to monstrous proportions, and to avert street accidents, but in the realm of psychic traffic, with its disproportionately greater dangers, very little is done to-day to defend humanity. The entreaty in the Lord's Prayer : " Lead us not into temptation ! " which is a mistranslation of the original " Lead us, when in temptation ! " receives very little regard. Apart from the prickings of conscience, everyone is at liberty to follow without let or hindrance any of the many roads leading to spiritual self-poisoning ; and so long as this state of affairs continues to exist, each one must be on his guard, and help himself and see to it that he is not hit or injured by the arrows of the wicked. In this psychic self-defence the auto-suggestion, " The surroundings in which I work and the people whom I meet, have no bad influence over me," will ward off the attack.

Here are a few rules which everyone should keep :

RISE EARLY AND PRACTISE PSYCHO-GYM-NASTICS !

EAT HARMLESS AND VARIED FOODSTUFFS !

EAT IN QUIET AND CHEW THOROUGHLY !

EARLY IN THE MORNING EAT DRIED FRUIT (PRUNES), IN ORDER TO ENSURE REGULAR ELIMINATION !

BE MODERATE IN EVERYTHING !

KEEP IN THE FRESH AIR AS MUCH AS POSSIBLE !

EVERYTHING THAT YOU UNDERTAKE, PERFORM WITH COMPLETE CONCENTRATION!

ALWAYS BE IN HARMONY—AND IN A GOOD HUMOUR, AND KEEP YOUR COMPOSURE IN THE MOST DIFFICULT SITUATION !

REORGANIZE YOURSELF

WHEN we leave the world of technical progress, in which industry has made use of rationalization, and turn our attention to the working of our own machines, we shall realize the great disproportion between technical development and our psychic backwardness. Our soul is like an oil lamp, which responds inadequately to present-day demands. When your watch ceases to work properly you take it without delay to a watchmaker, so that he can discover the reason for the irregularity and correct it. When you meet with vexation and failure, what do you do? Instead of finding out what is wrong with yourself and correcting it, you blame other people and curse fate. It would be better to say to yourself: "My psychic machine is running badly. It must be overhauled." One must not forget that to-day success is a fruit of science and not a winning ticket in a lottery. One should transfer rationalization from the realms of industry to psychic realms and endeavour to achieve the

best results with the least expenditure of
energy. We should rationalize our own
psychic machine, so that it works economically
and efficiently. For this purpose it is necessary
to eliminate all unnecessary speech and to
perform all ordinary actions, such as dressing,
etc., in the quickest possible time, and continue
in this way during the daily work. It is not
the place here to set forth all the practical
rules, which are imparted to each person
individually in the psychophonic technique
and system.

How should we behave in practical life?
Experience teaches that every great success
is based on a perfectly worked out, methodically managed and executed plan. The most
gifted army commander, even if he had the
best soldiers and ample supplies, could
achieve nothing, had he not formed a right
plan of campaign. Working according to
plan is to be recommended also for everyday
life, and we may take for granted that, without
a carefully thought out and comprehensive
plan, success in life is impossible. The victories
of Napoleon and Frederick the Great first took
form in their brains, and then took place on the
battle-field. Their thoughts became things.
In the same way we should always work out

our plan of campaign in our heads, and while doing this we should take note of the stages which lead to the desired goal, take account of our capacities and the means at our disposal, keep perpetually in view further aid, such as monetary assistance, and social contacts and everything else that may be helpful and advantageous, picture to ourselves the difficulties which we may encounter and try to foresee all possible surprises and attacks on the part of our opponents.

Psychophonic-life-conduct demands from us not only regard for the most important rules, but also claims from us at all times a positive attitude to life. When we meet an acquaintance on the street, let us greet him with the words, " I am pleased to see that you are so fit, and I expect to hear that you are doing well." Our first thought on waking should be that by reason of our self-confidence we feel full of new strength, and that everything will be easier and better for us. In the course of the day we should continually assure ourselves that we can easily overcome all troubles and vexations with the unused reserves of our inner forces. The most important thing is the way in which we react or behave in face of a sudden danger or unexpected misfortune, or when we

PSYCHO-GYMNASTICS TO THE PLAYING OF THE
ENERGY RECORDS

find obstacles in our way. It depends on us whether we react negatively or positively, that is, whether we despair or whether difficulties serve as a spur to increase our resisting power and enable us to overcome all difficulties. Modern psychology teaches us that our fate, as well as our psychic condition, is dependent only on ourselves. We are exactly what we think we are. In the worst situation it is not energy which we lack, but the positive attitude, which is needed to guide energy along the right track.

We insist that, in medical diagnosis, it is important to understand the whole human constitution, and to treat not only the body, but the soul, in mind and spirit, that is, the whole individual. And we have recommended to all readers of this thesis a return to psychic harmony, keeping in mind the slumbering and overwhelming forces within them.

Now we should like to return to a larger sphere and say with every emphasis : " Get back to God ! " " Unless ye become as little children, ye cannot enter into the Kingdom of Heaven." This does not mean that we are not to make any advance in our religious conceptions and outlook, and remain at the stage at which we were as children. One outgrows that in the same way in which one outgrows childish shoes and clothes, but we should guard against a thoughtless radicalism, and hasty jumping to conclusions. We can understand those who turn from the conception of the human-like deity of our childhood to the eternal Spirit of Love, but we blame strongly those who believe : " If God is not exactly what I thought Him to be when I was a small child, then there is no God."

We gain for the first time only when we are not contented merely with religious ideas and conceptions, but are actively connected with the eternal Spirit of Love, and develop the God within us more and more. Thus we assure an adjustment between ourselves and our surroundings, and comradeship and help of the most precious kind for our moral tasks and duties. For now God's power is in us, the weak ones *can* be mighty, no matter how steep the path before us. Because God Himself is carrying our load. God does not force Himself on anyone, but neither does He withdraw Himself from anyone who opens the door to Him. Get back to God ! and you will never fail or despair, but all the time exult with the apostle Paul : " If God is with us, who can be against us ? "

Dr. Cannon, in his remarkable book *Powers That Be*, writes as follows :

" Let us, then, deal with this process of imagination. Let us take a grip upon it and make it work for us, and for our health and our good. Let us see the law operating behind this faith-healing force of which we hear so much. Let us no longer look upon it as odd, or weird or peculiar. It is nothing of these. It is a real law, and a real force. There is only one way of dealing with the imagination, and that is to ' make-believe,' as it were. · We have to ' pretend ' that what seems to us unreal is actually very real. If we are ill we have to make health a reality to us. Only in this way will the forces of Life leap up in us and repair the damage to our body.

" How few people have realized the hidden meaning of Christ's great saying : Except ye become as little children, ye shall not enter into the kingdom of heaven. In other words, except you have enough faith to be able to see the good things about you and to believe them real, ye shall not attain to those good things. Did I not say in a previous lecture that this world is an illusion—a vision in a looking-glass, as it were ? Did I not tell you how a man may attain to the control of illusion ? Is not this faith-healing just that process ? Do we not control illusion and make our bodies conform to the perfect picture we hold in our mind ?

" The little child is perfect at making these illusions. It is an adept at ' let's pretend.' It unconsciously takes the first step in all creation —the control of the imagination.

" All the bad conditions prevalent in the world to-day are due to what may be called a disease of the imagination. We have allowed our imaginations to get out of our control, because nobody has believed the power that lies in them. Men have gone on believing that they may think anything they like in private, and that, so long as their thoughts are not known, they will be safe. Fools ! They have not realized that the unconscious mind holds a perfect record of every hidden thought and desire. They have not understood that their materialistic thoughts will ravage their bodies with disease, their nations with war, their businesses with depression, and their morals with corruption. They have not realized that in the unseen world they are heaping up for themselves a load of debt that cannot be paid except by suffering, or by repentance and reformation. Their imaginations have got out of their control, because they have not realized the need for guarding their action.

" Do not suppose that a man need hold definite thoughts of sickness in his mind to enable him to become sick. Not at all. It is enough for him to think of his body as a machine that is in danger of disease. The thoughts of sickness are implicit in the first thought and they will manifest. Therefore, it is not enough for a man to go through life with no control of his imagination. He must take himself in hand, otherwise, if he does not control himself, evil forces will do so. Your thoughts will become things, and a disordered mind will make a disordered life and a disordered body. Illness is not a positive thing, but a negation of wholeness. It is the result of bad thinking or of no thinking.

" What others make such a mystery of, I reveal to you as the result of a clear law. Therefore, tell yourself this fact over and over again. Do not get slack about it. As you concentrate upon it you will find your mind will more readily hold the right thought. Just as it becomes easier to swim or to ride a bicycle after much practice, so does it become easier to be a good liver by practice. School yourself to hold great thoughts. Make your imagination fasten upon good things, great things, noble things. Make a perfect picture of health in your imagination, and it will cause you to tune closer in to the harmonious wave-length of God. Health will come to you !

" People do not stop to realize that even the most materialistic among us really admit the truth of living on faith. The very man who proudly claims that he is ' a man of common sense, who has no time for faith,' will quite naturally pay his money into the bank and draw a cheque upon it because he has faith that the money will be credited to his account. ' Credited to his account'—why, the very word *credit* means faith, and it is quite the thing nowadays . . . to hear people say that the world lives on credit. If people would only carry their faith to the nth degree and believe in themselves, their God, and their fellow-men, we should leave the economic system to clear up itself ; for the political system, as the human system of man's body, lives by faith.

" You didn't create your own body, your parents did not create it either : they were merely agents for Life. Life created your body, and Life will heal it when it goes wrong if only you will open the way for Life by keeping your mind in the path of faith. You do not cause the wheat to grow, nor do you control the rains and the harvests, yet many of us believe that we can control our supply of God's good things. The truth is that if we only had faith in God we should not ' lay up for ourselves treasure on earth where moth and rust doth corrupt,' but we should ' lay up for ourselves treasure in heaven ' by having faith that next year will bring new harvests for distribution among all men. But men have no faith. They keep thinking fearful thoughts —what will happen to me to-morrow ? What will happen if another nation does this or that ? How shall I live if I lose my job ? This is entirely the wrong direction of your imagination. You should not concentrate upon morbid thoughts of that nature. You do not need to worry about to-morrow, or the minute after next, or the hour after next. All you need to do is to concentrate on *yourself* at the present moment : watching carefully that your own thoughts are right—*now* : being meticulous in the observance of the right attitude towards the problem of the moment : *thinking the right thing NOW : saying the right thing NOW :* and *doing the right thing NOW*, to the utmost of your ability.

" Work well and rest well—these are the secrets of success : and you cannot do either unless you have attained to that inner peace which faith in God alone can induce. When you work you should do what you have to do with all your heart and with all your soul. Do not slacken because you do not like your job. Visualize the sort of job you want to satisfy your ideal, but at the same time work all the harder at your present one. This will set the laws of life in motion and you will assuredly get the job you desire.

" I cannot impress upon you too forcibly the fact that all this depends entirely upon yourself. You want to be of some account in the world : in your profession : in your trade ! Begin to play-act the part. Live it ! Make it a part of yourself. It is up to you to begin to move the life-forces in your favour, for nobody else will do it for you. Imagine yourself as being what you want to be, and the faith behind this imaginative effort (for it is a supreme act of faith—creating in yourself the substance of things hoped for, as Paul says) will bring them to pass. The job you desired : the rank you wished to attain : the post you wanted to fill : the role you longed to act— all these will be yours if you act them in faith and in complete earnestness of purpose and with no levity in your mind. A word of warning to you in this respect, however. In gauging your own importance do not allow yourself to float along in a sea of superlative egotism. More commonly speaking, do not let your head swell. A proper estimate of oneself must include a survey of one's infinite task of self-development, and a clear understanding that the enormity of the task is no cause for regret or despair, but rather is a cause of great joy to think that one has such a clear road ahead of one, and such a clear law of progress along it. You must realize the relative nature of your position, and thereby retain a proper balance and a proper self-control. The more you realize your own importance, the more you will realize how frail you are except for the Life which is supporting you—the Life which is God. This realization will cool your self-esteem and put it into its proper place. It will show you that, as a son of God, you are bigger than you ever dreamed you could be, and you will find undreamed-of greatness and depths of power in yourself : but it will also show you that, as a ' lone hand ' fighting a supposedly lone fight against the universe, and puffed up with your own little

K

conceits, you are smaller than the poorest of God's creatures.

" We are surrounded by an etheric ocean in which the powers of thought move like lightning flashes from one mind to another. We are like complex instruments moving through a sea of power: our instruments flashing power to one another : being controlled by past influences from the power-house of memory to which all our instruments are tuned ; and to the power-house of custom (the collective mind) to which we are likewise attuned. Sometimes waves of adverse power come to us and cause our instruments to disintegrate. Sometimes this jarring effect spreads to others and causes an epidemic of jarring and of disintegration. Then we say there is a plague or an epidemic.

" But in the midst of all this chaotic action and reaction we have one haven of peace and strength that never changes. This is the great power-house of the universe : the great Universal Mind, God, the Creator of all things who rules His universe by telepathic control. We need only to tune our instruments to His wave-length, and then all the other jarring waves are blotted out and effaced by His peace which truly passeth all understanding.

" How do you tune into His wave-length ?
Why, I have been telling you all along ! Faith !
and again, Faith . . . faith that God is Good
and that all the host of Heaven and earth
must move to an increasing purpose when it is
consciously attuned to His power. Try it and
see the results. They are unfailing, for God
never fails us ! "

God moves in a mysterious way his wonders
to perform, and by psychophony, God has
developed through men a system to help all
who have already become accustomed to their
weaknesses and live with them. Drinkers,
smokers and all those afflicted with a psychic
weakness would rather live under the yoke of
slavery than break away and undergo an
efficacious cure by many methods, but this
method is acceptable to all.

My own nervousness spurred me to the
application of these methods. One day I said
to myself that I could live no longer with my
moodiness and obsessions, that I should prefer
death to a life without hope. Then I seized
the weapon of my psychic methods—and I
have victory—I have persevered. Persevered—
that is so easy to write, but how often I found
myself in the slough of neurasthenia before
I was at last able to step out into the sunshine
and a full life !

Each one of us is made for sunshine, laughter and happiness. Therefore, do not let us be our own executioners, and place tombstones over our lives. In all forms of nervous disorder let each one grasp the weapon of psychophony ; and not wait until we succumb completely to neurasthenia before we do this, but do it as soon as we suffer from depression. Everyone can go through life courageously and with bright eyes, and shape his future according to his wishes.

The secret of health, wealth and happiness, lies in successful frequent hetero-suggestion, as applied in psychophony. This golden secret is yours for the asking !

HAVE YOU BALANCED YOUR ACCOUNTS WITH LIFE ?

In general, man allows himself to drift with the tide, and it is very rare to find amongst our contemporaries a man who one day feels impelled to say to himself : " Now I have arrived at a point where I must reckon up all my revenues and expenditure in my psychic life."

We squander our energy and waste our time, and follow tactics in the conduct of our psychic life, which, if applied to matters less important than that of our lives, would infallibly lead to failure and ruin.

From time to time we should add up the totals of what we have received and what we have expended, in order to confirm exactly what is our profit or loss.

If we consider this operation quite a natural one when it concerns our material economy, why should we not do the same where our psychic life is concerned ? I have often asked myself this question, because, if we stop to reflect, we realize that our capacity for achieving gain and success depends, above all, upon our health, our energy and the rational and practical conduct of our life. This is why it is absolutely necessary that, from time to time, we take stock of our psychic condition by answering a questionnaire which we must set ourselves and answer with perfect sincerity.

Practical Hints

1. Apply your whole energy to the future and to your real aim

A man who to-day is an artist, to-morrow wishes to become an official ; and the day after to-morrow a merchant, who constantly changes his religious and political convictions, and who possesses no method, will never be master of his fate.

Impulsive or intermittent applications of will-power, outbreaks of enthusiasm, cannot take the place of systematic persevering work.

In this world nothing can be achieved without cost, and therefore the most important condition for success is diligence and perseverance.

Remember that you must work perpetually, not only until you have obtained the bare necessaries of life, but never cease until you are in a position to provide yourself with a certain degree of comfort, which is indispensable for a cultured man or woman.

This is only attained by those of strong character who know what they want and what they are striving for.

Do not fall into the trap of modern standardized organization and bureaucracy, but set yourself free from the enervating circle of those who straggle through life.

2. MAKE USE OF THE ENERGY WHICH CAN BE DERIVED EVEN FROM DISTRESSING EMOTIONS AND FEELINGS

In order to be able to keep oneself on the surface, one must understand how to transform the energy of despair, unhappy love and other negative feelings into positive ones. There are two ways of meeting the evil life has in store for us. Weak people submit themselves to it, sighing and grumbling ; others, on the contrary, the strong ones, transform every sorrow and misfortune in such a manner that they can use it to their own advantage.

In this way they charge their spiritual motor with fresh fuel.

Do you realize what enormous force there

is in the despair of someone who has lost someone near and dear to him ?

The same sense of loss which drives a weak person to despair or even suicide, inspires a strong-minded person, and endows him with strength to realize some great design or perfect a great work.

The gate that leads to the magic palace of our inner treasures and the storehouses of our energy is in the depths of our subconscious mind, and is so closely and firmly locked that it is often only a great misfortune or a deep sorrow which provides the key which will open it.

Therefore, be not like children who are afraid of pain. When sorrow approaches, let us welcome it as the forerunner of great deeds and creative energy.

Remember that the higher your position, the greater your responsibilities, the more exposed you will be to reverses and sorrows, and the better must you be prepared to overcome them victoriously.

3. HOW TO CULTIVATE RESISTANCE

When people meet with misfortune and grumble at their fate, they do not realize that what they consider to be ill-luck is often necessary for their success.

When they meet with heavy losses, they fail to recognize that if they meet their reverse in the right spirit it will release their latent energy, and enable them to win still greater fortunes.

4. IT IS SUFFICIENT TO BELIEVE THAT AN AFFAIR WILL TAKE A FAVOURABLE COURSE, IN ORDER TO ACHIEVE GOOD RESULTS

You will never achieve more than that which you believe you will achieve. One must firmly believe that in the future everything will take the happiest course, even if the outlook is as black as it can be. This applies above all to those losses which appear " irreparable " to us. In such cases you must convert the force of your emotions into work, and endeavour to fill your store of energy. In such a case it is best to attack, for never is attack more forceful than at the moment when we feel ourselves threatened on all sides and realise that the only possibility left to us is : To conquer !

Believe in your own strength and in victory, and be certain that your undertaking will succeed. Let your battle-cry be : " I can ! "

Be convinced that, no matter how big the reverse, you will rise to greater faith in yourself and your future.

5. A GOOD BUSINESS IS BASED ON MORAL PRINCIPLES

" Business " is not a matter of exploitation, speculation, swindling and sharp practice. In the opinion of Henry Ford one of the most essential features of real business is morality, i.e. the adjustment of business methods to those rules that are binding in the intercourse between individuals and nations. In this connection, he continues, there are many misunderstandings, false dealings and subterfuges. Many business men look upon morality as something unpractical, something that is thrown in as a make-weight, something for a holiday, that merely serves a decorative purpose. They believe that the deciding of what is good and bad, praiseworthy and blameworthy, is the business of religion and the churches, or at the most, dependent on the conditions of family and social life. They do not understand that judgment in the matter of what is good and bad, praiseworthy and blameworthy, is the very foundation of life, and also the basis on which all human relations are built, and that it must, therefore, also regulate business transactions. The public very soon find out when a banking business is dishonest, when houses are built on bad foundations, when goods are rubbish, when workmanship is poor, when a business is run by sweated labour or when usury is practised in any form or under any disguise. The public will soon find out such frauds and desert them, and sooner or later they are bound to end in bankruptcy and prison.

These wise ideas should guide every business man.

You must realize that in following the straight and narrow path you are in harmony with existing laws. Do not do this only with the expectation of finding a reward in the future life, but because you will also reap advantages from it in this life, and thus achieve permanent success.

From the point of view of modern psychology we can explain this as follows : A man whose dealings are always in keeping with moral principles can expect to obtain favourable results.

6. SUCCESS IS ENTIRELY DEPENDENT ON YOURSELF

In intercourse with your fellow men keep a certain distance. Avoid too great familiarity. No one will be able to see through you, and, for the reason that you appear incomprehensible to them, people will flock around the more thickly, for they will believe that there is some mystery connected with you. Everyone will wish to know you and to form a closer connection with you.

A man becomes just what he pictures himself in his own mind to be.

Question those who have achieved marked success, and they will always tell you that they think positively, that they always concentrate their thoughts on continual progress, and that they feel certain of final victory.

When you receive an important piece of news, do nothing hastily and endeavour not to betray in any way the impression it has made on you.

Everything that you have commenced carry out to the end.

7. PICTURE YOUR FUTURE TO YOURSELF AS YOU WOULD WISH IT TO BE

Everything must first mature in the mind before it bears fruit in the material world.

Even such an ordinary proceeding as the raising of a hand must first be performed in thought before it is transformed into an actual movement. This process can never take place in the inverse order.

The telegraph, the telephone, wireless telegraphy, the aeroplane and all other wonderful inventions were ideas first conceived in the brains of the discoverers.

The same applies to experience in our own lives.

Every business and every undertaking matures first in our spirit, then to be translated into a completed article, an organization or a transaction.

Therefore, if you wish to better your position or to take your place in a larger sphere of life, you must first experience this in spirit, and let your imagination paint a picture of it in bright colours.

8. THE ART OF WINNING THE BATTLE IN LIFE
   CONSISTS IN GUESSING TO WHAT EXTENT
   ONE'S OPPONENT IS WILLING TO YIELD

When you set out to do some work, or plan
a scheme, you must first not only weigh all
the pros and cons, but also turn your attention
to the people with whom you will have to
work.

Of what advantage is it if the cause is good
when the people with whom you work are not
trustworthy ?

If you wish to succeed, you must present
your plan in as advantageous a light as possible
in order to awaken in your partner the desire
to carry it out. You will be best advised to
adapt your proposals to his outlook on life and
understand how to put them in a form which
will attract him and appeal to his interests.

Before commencing business, make detailed
enquiries as to what is in greatest demand, so
that you will not find yourself in the position
of offering what no one wants. In making an
agreement the mistake is often made to take
for granted that conditions are permanent,
which instead are liable to change at any
moment.

Agreements should be as flexible as possible

and provide for every eventuality and possibility of change, so that you may avoid being taken by surprise.

Before accepting a business proposition, be cautious and make enquiries to ascertain exactly to whom it was previously offered, whether an attempt has been made to carry it out, and why it failed. Then consider carefully if you know of better methods than those used by your predecessor, and whether you possess the requisite means for carrying out the undertaking.

When an apparently advantageous financial proposition is put to you, do not lessen your clarity of vision by becoming excited, but apply your whole energy to strengthening your will-power. Analyse each proposal down to the smallest detail, until you arrive at its most essential factor. Assume that someone wishes to dupe you, and stipulate for such reservations and indemnifications as will enable you to withdraw from the business without loss.

Let us suppose that an inexperienced young man came to you for advice, saying : " I never have any luck. I can never keep the money I earn. Others always cheat me and take advantage of me. I lend money without demanding the usual guarantee. I sign bills of exchange

for people who have no security to offer and
then I commit myself to agreements without
having consulted a lawyer or an expert. I
know it is foolish, but I cannot say ' No ! ' "
Would not the reply be : " My dear sir, your
ailment is the result of lack of power to resist
those suggestions put to you by the people
you encounter on your way. In order to give
you the means of guarding yourself from
failure, I would advise you to do the following :
When someone makes you a business proposal,
repeat in your mind the following words,
' You have not the slightest influence over me.'
That will help you."

After a thorough analysis of the proposal,
after having pictured to yourself all possible
losses and disadvantages, and decided that it
is not suitable for you, you must politely but
firmly decline the proposal, without wasting
time on explanations and excuses.

9. YOU MUST BE A DIPLOMAT IN YOUR INTER-
COURSE WITH OTHERS

The man with a real knowledge of human
nature is he who possesses intuition, and so is
able to see so clearly into the life of another
that he almost becomes that person.

Over the entrance to the school for the knowledge of human nature the following inscription should be read :

" Always be accommodating in small matters.
Do not measure others' joy by your own."

The success of an undertaking is often decided by the tactics employed in human intercourse.

Adopt an attitude towards other people as if they were of no great importance to you, for then you will be able to disregard their words and behaviour and so gain a greater ascendency over them.

When anyone is talking to you, listen to him attentively, as if what you are hearing really interested you. From time to time reflect on whether you are in the presence of a real friend. Tear the mask from the face of those who pretend friendship, yet would betray you, so that they will never dare to try their false game again.

Know well whom you can trust and whom not. A true friend is he who has your interests at heart, as much as his own, who helps you to attain your goal, warns you of danger, and opens your eyes to details which may have escaped your notice.

L

Enemies—and who dare say that he has none —are there to act as a check on our sentimentality, and to make us alert to possible dangers.

Without enemies we should probably fall into a state of inactivity and slackness. If you possess powerful enemies, endeavour to make peace with them, unless your conscience— which should come before all material considerations—will not allow you to do so. Then avoid them until you feel more certain of yourself and can provide yourself with means for fighting.

Try to put your enemies off their guard, so that you can attack them suddenly, after you have thoroughly prepared your offensive.

When you notice faults and unpleasant traits in others, do not remark upon them, but learn from them what you should not be.

10. IMPROVE YOUR WORK DAY BY DAY

Whatever you may be, minister, workman, business man or official, see to it that your work improves day by day.

Be original in all you think and do.

If you notice that your business is showing symptoms of stagnation or decline, introduce new forms of advertising, think of a new name, place new and better samples on the market and adopt new trademarks.

At the same time give special care to your spiritual development and the improvement of your personality. You will then discover that not only the material end in view but also the spiritual fight to attain it will give fresh interests in life.

Life is perpetual movement and continuous progress, and for this you must fit yourself. A person who believes he can remain stationary will soon find that he is really slipping backwards.

11. LIFE IS A GAMBLE. THE PRIZE GOES TO THOSE WHO POSSESS COOLNESS AND INITIATIVE

Why does the professional gambler win most often ?

Because he plays according to a plan and remains cool.

In the game of life, as in a game of chance, calmness and self-control are essential, so that you may, when the right moment comes, have the courage to stake high. He who can say : " I have the power to resist, and can wait for a favourable result," will force fortune to smile on him.

After you have worked out your plan in every detail, watch carefully everything that is taking place, for even the smallest oversight may be sufficient to turn a successful issue into failure.

Every business and undertaking should be looked at and studied from all sides, in the same way as a responsible engineer will test every single part of a machine before passing it as fit for use.

12. PRAY DAILY FOR CHEERFULNESS, CONTENT-MENT AND SPONTANEOUS LAUGHTER

No one can abstain from food completely beyond a certain time without losing strength. Why should we deal differently with joy, cheerfulness and contentment, which are, after all, our spiritual nourishment ? Are you aware of the fact that these are more capable of strengthening the body and increasing our powers of resistance than the most nourishing food ?

Awake every day with a smile, and let the sunbeams of gladness fall into your soul. Is it really so difficult ? It is sufficient to think of something pleasant, to picture to yourself things of beauty, to cause the facial muscles to produce a smile, and to make the world appear in brighter colours, as if at the touch of a magic wand. Look for the pleasant and bright side of every affair, and let every impression, whenever possible, be a source of fresh pleasure to you. Make happy thoughts to bloom like flowers in your soul, and the world will reflect your mood and become a joyful place for you to live in.

13. LIGHT THE FLAMING TORCH OF SELF-CONFIDENCE

The more critical the situation in which you find yourself, the more must you concentrate your attention on success.

Positive thoughts attract favourable opportunities.

How often has it happened that people have lost their entire fortune and then have won it back again ! When everything seems at its blackest, lift your thoughts out of the present. If you look at the future with your spiritual eye properly focussed you will espy a rainbow, which is the forerunner of fine weather after the storm.

Often, when we think that the end of

everything has come, we suddenly find again the way we had lost.

How frequently does it happen that, when a man thinks his strength has completely left him, or his creative impulse is completely exhausted, he suddenly recovers his strength and self-confidence under the inspiration of some strong psychic stimulation.

14. AIM HIGH AND STRIVE TOWARDS A POINT BEYOND THE HORIZON

Is it not better to lead a creative life than to spend the uneventful existence of a human machine? Would you not prefer to fill a responsible post rather than be a clerk for ever and aye?

Have a high opinion of yourself. Make up your mind to become a leader.

Let your work be worthy of you, for then you have the right to demand much of fate. You are too great to take notice of the petty tricks by which fate tries to turn you from the path of progress. Let your imagination unroll at your feet the magnificent carpet of your career.

If your present post is only modest, and you wish to advance to something better, you must accustom yourself to seeing yourself in your mind's eye in the part you intend to play.

If in the past you have expended your energy on trifles and eking out a modest income, turn the same energy to larger undertakings.

Picture yourself in the company of the heads of finance and industry, and from imagining this intercourse acquire the strength required for perseverance.

If you really possess abilities, and therefore your work is better than what is demanded of you, why should you remain unnoticed, when others who are, perhaps, less able, take a prior place ?

Have courage to aim higher than you have hitherto done.

Steep yourself in the atmosphere of great undertakings.

If, when reading these words, you think of your own present poverty, at the same time remember that this moment is the best in which to mobilize your whole energy and aim at high as possible.

Do not be petty and miserly in smal matters.

It is much better to expend some money on enjoyment of a type which will increase your pleasure in work and inspire your creative impulse than to pile up money merely to gloat over its possession.

15. LET THE FOUNTAIN OF INTUITION AND CREATIVE ENERGY PLAY IN YOUR SOUL

How necessary it is to withdraw oneself for a time from the hubbub of modern life, in order to devote ourselves to contemplation, to reflect about ourselves, and to examine our relation to our surroundings, to our work and to our fellow creatures.

When we look deep into our innermost soul we approach God, until we become one with Him, and are enabled to see everything in its true proportions. And, behold, we find ourselves on a spiritual island, far removed from the worries and cares of material life.

Into this seclusion you must retire whenever you have to solve some momentous problem, just as the priests and prophets of old went into the solitude of the " wilderness " when they wished to commune with their God and prepare themselves for great deeds.

Where is this magic island ?

It lies in the depths of our subconscious mind, there where the eternal flame of our

THE POWERFUL EFFECT OF THE RELAXATION RECORD
Note one girl already fast asleep in her chair.

immortal ego burns, where the treasure-
chamber of our vitality, energy and creative
power is to be found.

16. THE ELIXIR OF THE SPIRIT

Let us now talk of your leisure hours.

It is imperative that you should have a
well-ordered, regular life, on workdays as
well as holidays, in which time is set apart for
work and for study, for enjoyment and for
idleness.

" Study ? " you ask. " I have left school
long ago."

And yet, reflect. From the moment of your
first independent thought, yes, even earlier,
from your first impressions of faces and
sounds, ideas began to form in your mind.
The mechanism of your spiritual powers,
your abilities, and your will gradually grew
stronger and took definite shape.

What causes the change which turns a child
into a man or woman ?

It is the influence of environment. It ripens,
enriches and destroys the soul.

Has your everyday life a beautiful back-
ground ? Is it the open country or a crowded,
artificial town ?

Is it the society of your fellow men ? Let them be always active, talented and useful men and women. Then their society will irradiate you with strength and self-confidence.

Finally, the other daily companions you should have—books.

What books are you to read ?

Do you ever read poetry or essays ?

The increasing materialistic trend of modern life has unfortunately decreased the number of those who seek and find pleasure and inspiration in the reading of poems or beautiful prose, and opened the flood-gates to a never-ending stream of cheap literature ; novels, detective stories and so-called " thrillers," most of which lack those noble characteristics which alone can make books worth reading.

And as it is with literature, so it is with painting, sculpture, music and the theatre.

If you give yourself the trouble to think deeply over what you read, see or hear, do you not come to the inevitable conclusion that the general trend is towards the cultivation and glorification of what is base and ugly ?

Books and plays in which licence, crime and brutality are described and even exalted, until we come to regard them as natural. Statues and paintings which are ugly in conception and execution ; distorted and base. Music which purposely replaces melody and harmony by discords and shrieking confusion of noises ; symphonies which are nothing but cacophonies ?

The truth is that all this perverted art is the synthesis of our mode of living, unnatural, restless, distressed, depressed, feverish, confused, lacking in noble ideals and real beauty. And while for this reason it appeals to the majority, it has the effect of a harmful drug and perverts their minds still further.

All these influences you must avoid. They are a deadly poison.

There are good books, if you will but take the trouble to find them. Not only the old classics, but modern writings. There are noble works of art for you to contemplate. There is good music for you to hear. Seek and cultivate beauty and idealism. Refuse to contemplate, read, or listen to, anything that is ugly.

Then literature and art will lift you into higher spheres, purify and ennoble you, guide you and support you, and above all strengthen you to remain high above all the man-made drabness and dullness and ugliness of life, and live in the sunshine of the beauty of life which is God's work and which you will often rejoice to find where you least expect it.

And do not forget to look for it within yourself, until you have found the divine spark that is in every human being.

Let this quest form a part of your daily routine. It will give you untold strength to march on the path which out of chaos will lead you to happiness.

17. THE OLD DREAMER DIES, THE NEW MAN OF FORCE AND ACTION ARISES

Your hour has struck. It is time that you should make practical use of our advice, and prove its worth. A man who does not practise what he preaches is not a real man, but only a shadow.

Socrates, Aristophanes, Epictetus, Napoleon and Ford were great because they understood how to transform their principles and ideas into action, and how to apply them to life.

I consider Henry Ford to be the greatest practical philosopher of our time.

His exceedingly simple system may be described as follows :

Everyone of us can achieve material

independence in life. This is entirely dependent on our own work, will-power and self-confidence. It is necessary to concentrate our whole energy on our tasks, to show daily increase in our activity, and endeavour always to improve our work.

This modern philosopher applied his system to practical life and thereby amassed an enormous fortune.

Victory will only go to those who have succeeded in attaining perfect harmony between spirit and body. The body must keep in step with the spirit, and every idea will become action. Hold your head high, and ceasing to be the slaves of institutions, traditions and routine, introduce harmony between yourself and them.

In this way you will win back your personal independence and will live a full life of your own.

Only those can gather the magic flower of happiness who develop their abilities to the highest degree, and continue to cultivate them industriously. This must be your aim of life.

Let your thoughts rise as high as the stars, when you are working for a noble purpose. Looked at from this height, drab, everyday existence loses its ordinary aspect and all petty complications disappear like morning mist.

Is there anything finer than to be conscious of having control of life, and of being able to subdue fate, as one tames a wild, untrained horse ?

Become master of your life, grasp the rudder energetically and you will arrive safe and confident at your goal, even if you have had to weather the worst storm.

Epicurus, the most ardent disciple and devotee of life, overthrew the gods, and ordered life itself to be worshipped as a deity.

" Our life," he said, " is the only one we possess. Therefore we should use it to the best advantage every day, and worship it in gratitude."

Be honest with yourself. Long for joy in life as you long for the sun.

Say " Yes ! " to life at every step, and at life's altar worship joy as the highest of all moral values.

If there is one amongst you who does not understand this inner divine voice let him listen to the singing of birds rejoicing in the coming of spring, look at the starry heaven on a clear summer's night, or listen to the mysterious murmuring of the waves of the unfathomable ocean ; then he will feel so near to the heart of nature that he will awake from the terrible nightmare that has troubled him up to now.

All advice and commands given in this book have the purpose of rousing the will to power in those who are weak, discouraged or embittered. In psychophony I have set forth the system of exercises which serve this end. Life should be treated as a business, as a contract with the present and a guide for the future.

Not for one moment have I had the intention of deceiving the reader in this matter, of leaving him to believe that these thoughts will give him complete contentment, take him straight to his goal and guide him into the haven of happiness. I need fear no contradiction when I say that apart from what I have said, it is necessary that the real, unspoken suppressed wish be expressed, penetrates to the depths of the heart and there finds the hidden gold. It is necessary that the longing waiting for fulfilment be expressed, and realized in the depths of the spirit.

The realization of this must include also the understanding that fortune, position, honours and worldly powers are illusions, false values of everyday life and quickly pass beyond recall.

They are good, in fact often indispensable as means to an end, but are not an end in themselves. Imagine for a moment that you possess everything. What would happen? Your days and nights would be one long weariness. There would be nothing left to strive for.

You will only be able to live again, recover your strength and vitality when the star of idealism shines brightly. Only then will life reach its highest significance. Man is then freed from trivialities, and strives for no one's favour. He pauses in his race for money, knowing that he cannot take it to the grave with him. To work for an ideal gives to everyone the contentment of a noble, luminous, incomparable reality.

What ideals are these?

Where are they to be found?

Indian æsthetes see life's aim at fusion with God, with the Infinite.

Have you seen them portrayed? They sit with bowed head on the ground and think. Of what do they think? Nobody knows. Months and years go by. Grass has grown upon the filth of their bodies, their limbs have become atrophied, their eyes have become dull, vermin teem in their matted hair and are picked out by passing birds. Yet the æsthete perseveres in his stony silence and unites his spirit with his God. The disciples of the sect, worshippers of his passive suffering, put particles of food between his withered lips to sustain his body. It is a pitiable fate.

This man's attitude is wrong.

For years he has indulged in voluntary suffering. On looking at him, we can but grieve for the wasted energy of this man, of his good intentions, and of the love he lavishes on his illusions.

Far be it from me to point at such a goal for you.

Your goal must be action, but the action of work in a life within the community. There are plenty of opportunities for such work.

There are more of them than there are stars in heaven, if one only raises one's eyes above the commonplace.

Let us take, for example, science and art.

You will answer that you are neither a scientist nor an artist, and that you have neither talent nor inclination for these vocations.

You are right. Without the divine spark

M

which is commonly called " talent," you only waste paper and canvas.

Politics, perhaps, then ?

That is a game of the ambitious, of class interests, of intrigues, and is often associated with unclean methods. Politics are apt to frighten and disgust those who are not disposed to compromise.

Would you be inclined to devote yourself to social work ?

" There are others to do that," you answer.

That, however, is no valid reason. Wherever you are, there is a communal life, at every step you find how much there remains to be done. In the development of culture, in the practice of charitable works, and even in sports, which, pursued reasonably, are healthy training for the benefit of nation and humanity.

Always be more interested in something outside of your own self. Do not work exclusively for your own advantage, and you will be amply rewarded.

It is not difficult to find the right way.

You can read in every newspaper news of the activities of cultural and humanitarian societies. There are countless societies which have for their object the general weal.

Unite your efforts with those of others.

Become, like them, a builder of the general good. Learn yourself, and teach others. Endeavour to give to the future what the past gave you for your benefit. Do not think that your help in association with others is of too little value, and is insufficiently productive. In the mechanism of existence every little cog plays its important part in the development and progress of humanity.

Charity !

Not the penny that one throws to the beggar in the street, often in order to be rid of his importunities. But practical sympathy with helpless orphans, the weak and aged, with uncomplaining poverty, with cripples. During the War, the wounds crying to be healed in hundreds of hospital wards led many idle women, accustomed to a luxurious and sheltered life to join the ambulance service.

The War is over, almost forgotten. But poverty, sickness and pain are still crying for help and pity.

For understanding eyes, for a sympathetic heart, the scope for work here is as wide as the ocean.

Everyone can, according to his means, contribute to the general good, the power, glory and unity of his nation, and the reputation

and significance of his family and his name.
No one can tell whether or when his efforts
will meet with outside recognition and reward.
But the knowledge that he has fulfilled his
duty towards mankind will give him a pure
and exalted emotion, which the poet felt when
he exclaimed : " Men, soon you will be like
gods."

No matter to what sphere of society you
belong, whether you are a labourer or a
magnate, a simple man or a scholar, a child
or a greybeard, you can give vent to the most
noble elements in your soul, in your relations
with your environment, as in your relations
with unknown and far-distant people.

Distribute love all around you.

Work—place yourself at the service of
humanity, regardless of the cost to you, and
of material returns.

There are countless examples.

Think of the genius of many true artists,
who are not concerned with material gain,
live in poverty, and yet never lose their
sense of humour. Whose life is happiness and
laughter.

Think of explorers, facing unknown dangers
and privations, physicians and scientists, many
of them martyrs, joyfully offering their

thoughts, their time, their blood and their life to an idea which is part of a priceless treasure which belongs not to them, but to the whole of humanity.

Every good deed is a gift, a contribution to the happiness of the world in general.

It reacts upon the giver and enriches his spirit.

Life, if you can but see it in the right light, is a priceless gift. You have received it. Use it in the right way. Not selfishly and meanly, but for others and lavishly. Not gloomily, but joyfully. Help to make this world not a world of tears, but of happy laughter.

18. IMAGINARY EXCURSIONS

We should practise making excursions from drab everyday life into fairyland, but instead of travelling on a magic carpet, as in the *Arabian Nights*, we should travel on the wings of our own imagination.

When evening falls and you have an hour of leisure, close your eyes, and allow all that is dormant in the subconscious mind to rise to the surface—all your suppressed wishes, all that you longed for as a child, will appear in the moonlight of your imagination, and come to fulfilment. Live, in your imagination, your own fairy tales. Quench your inward thirst, and set free all imprisoned secret wishes and dreams.

19. PSYCHOPHONIC " SAVOIR VIVRE "

There is a great art in behaving nobly in a humiliating situation, or in preserving the calm and confidence of a victor when in an unfavourable position.

Just as one is able to recognize a gentleman by his bearing, so is it possible to recognize a personality by his behaviour in danger, in moments of emotional stress and in sudden misfortune.

In the spiritual storeroom of Psychophony are to be found not only the fuel of natural ambition and self-confidence, but also the various lubricants to ensure smooth working of our lives, such as perseverance, fortitude, energy, altruism and joyfulness.

20. A SPIRITUAL WEEK-END

At least once a week one should withdraw from the noise of the city and daily life into the silent depths of one's soul. Sunday would be the most suitable day for this, when nothing will disturb you while you inhale the pure air of positive thoughts, as if they were the fragrance of pine trees, and yield yourself up to peace and quiet until you feel that you are in harmony with the Infinite. You will then be permeated with a feeling of strength and confidence.

Your inner calm will be like the mirror of a motionless lake, and you will drink from the crystal-clear spring of natural joy in life.

21. THE ISLAND OF BLISS

The perpetual striving to heap up material possessions and the increase in production have brought about collapse. The present crisis has shown this and has proved the bankruptcy of the modern mechanical age. Slowly people are beginning to realize that true happiness is based on a feeling of contentment and harmony, and the time will come when people will also see that altruism is really only a properly comprehended and applied egoism. To-day the value of morality is becoming more and more recognized. To dedicate oneself to the service of others only, to work for charity and make others happy means that you make yourself happy.

Instead of overworking yourself like some of the insatiable, great and notorious financiers of the post-War period, whose nerves were so overstrained that they were inevitably over-taken by disaster, would it not be much better to take the other road of self-control and self-victory ?

Instead of trying to satisfy ever-increasing desires, wish for less, so that you can look into the show-window of life and long only for those things in the display which are necessary for a cultured person.

Picture to yourself the many sensual pleasures in which countless thousands seek diversion or forgetfulness from the haunting fear of their outer or inner lives.

Visualize, for instance, a hall filled with people who, deprived of their powder, paint and finery, would shock you by their white and strained appearance, by the haggard ex-pression of their eyes, the tired expression of their bodies, which they whip to activity and faked brightness by drink and other stimu-lants. Watch them how they dance in the smoke-laden air, or sit at the tables, engaged in empty talk or bored to death. And compare this with life in the open, in God's free nature —whether it be in bright sunshine or in the majesty of a raging storm, in the warmth of a mild day or the cold of clean, white silent snow. Think of quenching your thirst at a crystal-clear spring. . . . Which would you prefer ?

This example is given to illustrate life in general and your attitude towards it. It is largely a matter of being able to recognize what is real and worth having, and what is fake and not worth having. On that ability the worthiness of our own life depends to a large extent.

What we all seek is happiness. But happiness is a purely spiritual matter. It depends entirely on our mental attitude whether a certain thing, a certain event, a certain achievement will make us happy or not. And according to whether we are able or not to distinguish true beauty and harmony, real worth and real merit from apparent beauty, false worth and fictitious merit, our happiness will be real and lasting or false and ephemeral.

There are, however, many things which cloud or distort our power of vision. Our eyes are nothing but a camera, which projects the picture of what we see on to a nerve tissue, the retina. But this picture becomes reality to us, not in the eye, but in our brain, in our mind.

And just as it is with our ocular vision, so it is with our spiritual vision. The " seeing," the realizing of what is not material and the detecting of the spiritual aspect of material things and their consequent valuation. If there are things in our minds which cloud or distort this spiritual vision, we can never be happy and we can never be successful.

Need I tell you what these impediments to true vision and appreciation, to happiness and success are ? You know them : fear, worry, shyness, lack of self-confidence, despondency, melancholia, and all the other troubles of which I have spoken in this book.

The troubles which lurk in your subconscious mind and which Psychophony can cure.

If you understand this you will also understand why such an eminent authority as Dr. Alexander Cannon, whose deep knowledge of psychology is undisputed, wrote what follows :

" BEXLEY,
KENT.
14th March, 1935.

I have a very intimate knowledge of the research work which Dr. Radwan has been doing. In my opinion it is of the utmost importance that this research be continued in this country.

My investigations of the methods and technique adopted satisfied me beyond all reasonable doubt that here we have a most valuable national asset, in that by its use normal people can prevent mental and physical fatigue, double their efficiency and prevent mental and nervous breakdowns. I have also observed its great value in the treatment of certain forms of mental and nervous disease, results far exceeding any known in this country. Even cases of organic disease which have a large functional accompaniment are benefited thereby.

I know of medical and other men of eminence in this country who are using experimental records with special suggestions produced thereon by a special Dr. Radwan technique, and have already found the method of great value in the training of their children.

Of Dr. Radwan I can also speak personally, and I consider him a scientist of undoubted ability and one whose probity is unquestioned.

ALEXANDER CANNON, K.C.A.
M.D., PH.D., D.P.M., M.A., F.R.G.S."

GUIDING PRINCIPLES

THE Radwan system of psychophonic treatment is based on the following guiding principles :

1. Science and technique have not only made it possible to reproduce speech and music by mechanical means, but also to convey by the same means the effects which such speech or music makes upon the human mind. Why, then, should it not be possible to transmit suggestions and psycho-gymnastics by mechanical means of the same kind ?

2. Our nature longs for harmony. Instead of asking ourselves how success and happiness may be obtained, we should ask how we can free ourselves from adverse influences and our repressions, so that we may be able to realize ourselves fully.

3. That which prevents the full development of our talents and our taking advantage of them is not lack of energy but its false application.

4. Scepticism destroys our faculty of influencing ourselves, therefore the individual is not able to influence himself and requires a mechanical stimulus, just as a motor engine requires a starter.

5. Psychophonic technique sets in motion the latent psychic powers of our mind, so that we may use them to our practical advantage in all that concerns our daily life.

THE END

47

84 - proof.

ƒƒpƒ. pood sestesce

Bƒ book

Printed in the United States
100041LV00008B/259/A